ONE  FLAT
COYOTE
ON THE CENTRE LINE

For
Kathleen Wheler and Selma Goa
with love

ONE FLAT COYOTE
ON THE CENTRE LINE

Cruising Canada
in a classic Chevy

KAREN GOA

First published in 2006 by New Holland Publishers (NZ) Ltd
Auckland • Sydney • London • Cape Town

www.newhollandpublishers.co.nz

218 Lake Road, Northcote, Auckland, New Zealand
14 Aquatic Drive, Frenchs Forest, NSW 2086, Australia
86–88 Edgware Road, London W2 2EA, United Kingdom
80 McKenzie Street, Cape Town 8001, South Africa

ISBN-13: 978 1 86966 120 5
ISBN-10: 1 86966 120 6

Managing editor: Matt Turner
Editor: Alison Dench
Design: Dee Murch
Cover design: Nick Turzynski, redinc.
Illustration: Fraser Williamson

A catalogue record for this book is available from the
National Library of New Zealand

10 9 8 7 6 5 4 3 2 1

Colour reproduction by Pica Digital Pte Ltd, Singapore
Printed in China at Everbest Printing Co

CONTENTS

Acknowledgements

A whole countryful of Canadians deserves my heartfelt gratitude, especially our families and friends old and new, who nurtured us and the Beast across the nation.

Special thanks to Bruce Brotzel, without whom there'd have been no car, no trip and no story. Let's do it again sometime, eh? Also to my sister Colette Wheler, for lending Bruce and her own hands to the cause.

Much love to Kathleen and Gordon Wheler, and Selma and Elmer Goa, for love and support far beyond the call of parenting fifty-year-olds.

Sharon Phillips Ridley and John Mannering, thanks for keeping the faith. Happy cruising.

Thanks to the supportive and clear-sighted team at New Holland, in particular Belinda Cooke, Matt Turner and Dee Murch, and to Alison Dench for her thoughtful editing.

And last but never, ever, least, my eternal love and gratitude to Ken, my husband and driver par excellence, for his unconditional love, special humour and hundreds of patient U-turns via manual steering. Without you I would walk a lonely road.

In this book the names of some people have been changed.

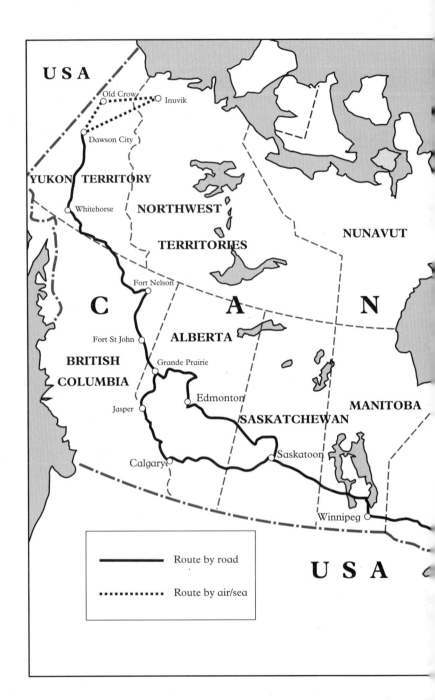

USA

Old Crow○⋯⋯○ Inuvik

○ Dawson City

YUKON TERRITORY

NORTHWEST

○ Whitehorse

TERRITORIES

NUNAVUT

Fort Nelson ○

C   A   N

Fort St John ○   ALBERTA

BRITISH   ○ Grande Prairie

COLUMBIA

○ Edmonton

Jasper ○   SASKATCHEWAN   MANITOBA

Calgary ○   ○ Saskatoon

Winnipeg ○

USA

─────── Route by road

⋯⋯⋯⋯ Route by air/sea

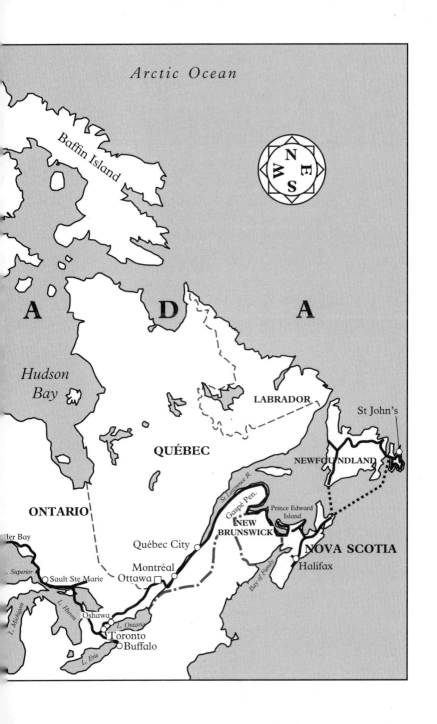

Prologue

The Chevy wallowed in a gruesome stain sprung from its ancient innards. Primer-patched and furred with rust, the old brown and white mongrel hunkering in my parents' Saskatoon garage needed a quiet lie-down in a corner, not a forced march across Canada.

'It's so – fifties. A real old – classic. Look at all that chrome.' Stuck for words, I clutched at the wretchedly obvious.

'All that rusty chrome.' Ken, my driver-husband and soon-to-be panel beater, poked the thing in the flank. A tarnished flake fluttered away. 'Feck. What have we done?'

Bought a classic car, sight unseen, over the Internet, that's what. Some advice for anyone thinking of doing the same: throw the laptop out the window and handcuff yourself to the nearest heavy object until the urge passes. What were we thinking?

Sleek curvy lines and chrome bumpers, sassy tail fins and dual exhaust. The unbridled V8 power of a Detroit thoroughbred. That's what we were thinking. Celebrating Ken's fiftieth birthday cruising across Canada in a car of similar vintage sounded, in the laziness of a New Zealand summer, like a special but not too strenuous way to see parts of our homeland we'd missed while living there, and revisit some favourite spots. Not for us a Samoan sun-worshipping session or sipping wine under a Tuscan sky. It had to be a road trip.

My beloved and I are high school sweethearts. We met in a friend's 1956 Pontiac. Ken soon bought a kick-butt '65 Chevrolet Impala, throbbing with crimson under-dash 'sex lights' and a rocket-like exhaust system. I was so impressed I married him.

A handful of years later I awoke once too often in the wintry Saskatchewan blackness to the radio announcer's Voice of Doom:

'The temperature is minus thirty-two degrees. This is minus fifty-five degrees with the wind chill. Exposed flesh freezes in less than one minute.' Another day of plugging in the car's electrical block heater to coax the engine oil from solid to slippery. Another bundled-up midnight trudge in a blizzard across a bleak hospital car park at the end of my shift in the hospital's pharmacy, only to find the car doors frozen shut and the tyres ice-cube square. We fled Saskatchewan's prairies for fewer clothes and new jobs in warmer, greener New Zealand.

Many things downunder delighted us: the soft winters, nikau palms and tree ferns on hillsides, the briny scent of the sea, the starry Southern Cross and the accents, so lovely on Kiwis, so much like a sheep choking on a cabbage when I tried to imitate it. But cars had shrunk. Our first car was a dispirited 1978 Ford Escort sedan, really just a guinea pig on wheels but less courageous.

On the prairies it's a long way to anywhere. Driving as a leisure activity is a birthright, starting right at birth. No guinea pigs disguised as cars need apply. On sunny Sundays in Saskatoon my parents piled their brood into the back of a '47 Buick convertible and drove us to the Diamond Grocery, near the Honeybunch Bakery, for ice-cream cones. In teenage years riding around all night in '56 Pontiacs or '65 Chevys with teenage boys, eight-track tapes endlessly looping Deep Purple or Uriah Heep, was what teenage girls did. 'Let's go for coffee' sometimes meant 'Let's drive three hours to Regina'. On one long weekend Ken and I drove 1600 kilometres through the Rocky Mountains to Vancouver, visited some friends, got up the next morning and drove 1600 kilometres back again.

Let's be clear: Ken drove. I passengered. Marital relations are better that way.

On this Canadian road trip we didn't intend to put selves and classic car through such gruelling paces. Fifty is not the new fifteen. Our plotted route ran north-west from Saskatoon on the Yellowhead Highway, north along the World Famous Alaska Highway to the Yukon Territory's old gold-mining towns, then back down through the wild beasts and brawn of the Rocky Mountains, across British Columbia all the way to Vancouver's street scenes and nightlife. There we planned to dip a ceremonial toe in the Pacific Ocean, turn around and cross the entire continent to dip the same toe in the Atlantic Ocean in wind-blasted Newfoundland, the most easterly of the nation's provinces and last on the list of must-see places.

After twenty years of ex-pat life I was keen to see if our native land was still familiar, or wonderful, or strange. I looked forward to the odd chat with ordinary Canadians, those polite, fair and law-abiding folk much like, well, ourselves, unless either we or they had changed. An amble across prairie, over mountains, to the sea, stopping to sample the cuisine and check the oil; all this fitted into the plan to buy classic car, drive and camp in classic car, sell classic car. It sounded simple. We should have known better.

A decade earlier we'd toured Europe for a summer in a smart-looking Ford Escort van snapped up for £150 from a South London used car salesman who saw us coming, fresh off the plane and glinting wetly behind all four ears. Barely wide enough for two thinnish campers to doss down in the back (with the rear door left ajar for Ken's feet to stick out), the baulky British-made heap flatly refused to start at the slightest hint of damp in the air, there being no damp in Britain.

For four months I pushed and Ken jump-started this shonky piece of business through France (where the country folk pointed and laughed), Spain (where they laughed but helped push), Portugal (where they gathered in knots and lamented) and finally into Italy (where they milled about exclaiming and pressed glasses of wine upon us). We sputtered into a Roman campground and slapped a For Sale – As Is, Where Is sign on the van. A day later a tattooed Czech ex-gangster traded £10 for the keys. True to his born-again Buddhist teachings, when the starter motor blew up only hours after money changed hands he didn't reach for a sharp blade but merely looked thoughtful. (He *had* been warned.) We jumped on a train to Brindisi on Italy's heel and escaped on a boat to Athens before he suffered a criminal relapse.

After the cramped, cranky miseries of the Ford, driving and sleeping in a five-metre long, two-metre wide Chevy station wagon would be luxury. The problem was how to buy a decent, reliable North American classic car from half a planet away in Auckland.

'Check out the Internet,' emailed brother-in-law Bruce from Saskatoon. 'I buy stuff online all the time.'

Neither of us had ever bought as much as a spark plug over the Internet. Still, millions of buyers had, and were the happier for it. Virtual tyre-kicking began in earnest; ads for Chevys in Arizona, California, Alabama (there were no Canadian candidates) fell into our inbox courtesy of Bruce. Under this relentless barrage we targeted a 1956 Chevrolet 210 Townsman station wagon a little closer to Canada, in Washington state. The car looked a bit tired but sounded like just the thing to take us cross-country for three months. 'Good, solid mechanics,' the description said, 'tracks straight, very superficial rust, requires very little prep for painting. Runs and drives beautifully, very dependable.' Bruce supplied helpful hints to us online virgins. We bid furiously on the car. Seconds before the auction ended we snatched it away from slower, less canny bidders.

The plan was to fly into Seattle in May and pick up our classic wagon. From there we'd jaunt across the US-Canada border to the nearest lakeside campsite, rhinestone sunglasses sparkling and 'Leader of the Pack' playing on the radio. But as January turned to February, the four-month gap before we were to take possession of this car started niggling. Maybe there wasn't a car at all – maybe it was an Internet hornswoggle.

Bruce was just as anxious to see the Chevy safely in Saskatoon. He offered to fetch the car back on a test trip across the US-Canada border, over the Rocky Mountains and through three provinces. This was a great plan: Bruce is a top notch mechanic who loves old cars.

The legalities, I was confident, would be easy. In London we'd paid a paltry sum to a small grey clerk in a small grey inner-city bolthole. In return he'd given us a piece of green paper confirming we owned the Ford van and were free to travel wherever, whenever and with whomever we liked. But that was there, and this was somewhere else.

First the good news. A car half a century old needed no grunty bumpers, air bags or other modern safety features to enter Canada. US border officials wanted three days' notice of its leaving their territory, for reasons known only to them, but other than that, no problem. Then the bad news. As non-residents we couldn't register the car in Saskatchewan. Yes, emailed the nice lady at Saskatchewan Government Insurance, under special secret circumstances (no doubt involving the full moon and maybe some bloodletting) non-residents could register a car temporarily. But don't even think about taking it out of the province. I envisaged government-issue electronic dog collars round our necks and a disabler for the car that zapped us all when we approached Saskatchewan's borders.

'You may have to take a leap of faith and give that nice car to a trustworthy Saskatchewan resident,' mused Bruce from afar. 'I've always wanted a classic Chevy.'

Done. Bruce promised not to lay claim to the car after we'd finished 'borrowing' it. We promised not to rack up a bunch of speeding tickets in his good name. Then Bruce needed form K22 from Canadian customs to import the car. Plus show his driver's licence and the title at the border. Plus pay seven per cent goods and services tax on the spot; another whacking seven per cent provincial sales tax came later. Plus do a funky chicken dance while singing the national anthem and swear to officials on both sides of the border that neither he nor the car nor any of his blood relatives had any dodgy Colombian connections. All of this he did.

The car, though, tracked as straight as a drunken hay wagon. It veered instead of steered. Bruce, who is not a cowardly sort, abandoned our expensive new purchase in the mountain town of Golden, British Columbia, lest it pitch into an uncontrollable skew and toss him down a crevasse. He bought a bus ticket home.

'Car is not roadworthy and is dangerous to drive,' thundered Bruce by email, at the end of a long and expensive-looking list of 'Things Wrong with Car'. A month later the car arrived filthy and snow-blown in Saskatoon, not under its own 305 cubic-inch V8 steam, but in ignominious defeat on the back of a truck.

Over the next few months I sent large cash injections to Bruce. The Chevy's many defects so offended him he rolled up his sleeves and knocked it into roadworthy shape, popping up from under the car to send depressingly frequent emails spelling out its faults.

'Positive battery cable to starter is jammed against engine block. This could burn up car.'

'Wrong carb for transmission and carb has other problems. Work work work money money money.'

'Having real problems getting the windshield wiper on the passenger side to work. You may have to travel with squeegee kid or small woman with long, skinny arms and many joints.'

Then, at last: 'Steers well stops well. Come and get it.'

Beast is a Burden

SASKATCHEWAN 56
164·436
WHEAT PROVINCE

' We're going on a road trip, not to jail. '

Ken, driver, Saskatoon, Saskatchewan

Despite its flea-bitten look the car, dubbed, not fondly, 'the Beast', did start, steer and stop well. Bruce, though, was a weary, beaten man, greasy-knuckled and cracked nearly in half from months of crawling around under the car manhandling motors, brakes and drive trains. But he still had enough spark left in him to wheeze, 'New hub caps would look good. You can get some on the Internet.'

Fergawdsake. Did he think we'd learned nothing at all about online auctions?

Most of my family still lives in the neat, green university city of Saskatoon, spread along the South Saskatchewan River. We usually visit in summer. I'd forgotten about spring. Spring in Saskatoon smells of sweet lilac and honeysuckle, mown lawns and wild roses. Garter snakes sun their stripy selves along the riverbank. Beavers nibble. Muskrats dive. Gophers, that pesky rodent nuisance, spawn more gophers. It's a fertile, frisky time of year.

But this foul-tempered spring was in no rush to move on. Tornadoes and baseball-sized hail battered the south; floods washed away trailers and cars in the east, and drowning deluges in neighbouring Alberta had churned the river into a surging monster of a thing downstream in Saskatoon.

'I hope you've got your oars ready,' said Bruce.

Ken missed all of this. At night he slept like a dead thing. The rest of the time he retreated to the garage-cave, emerging only to blink at the light, whimper, and slink back into the dimness. He slumped through the door at the end of each day of sandblasting rust from the Beast's mangy hide pale as a floured ghost and muttering dark and savage oaths.

'How'd it go?'

'Mutter mutter feck you don't want to know mutter.'

Bruce had done a five-star job of improving the car's mechanics from dangerous to drivable. It had the odd quirk, like starting in any gear, including reverse. But the Beast threw money-gobbling hissy fits almost daily. As a welcoming gesture the heater core blew up. On day two the tailgate window spontaneously imploded in a zillion pieces.

'I had the same thing happen once with a giant pickle jar,' said my sister Colette, Bruce's partner.

The Beast had sniffed out our plan to drag it across the entire country. It was old, tired and did not want to go. We tried to remain cheerful. The alternative was descent into gibbering madness.

Buying a '56 Chevy gave us access to the Chevy brethren of North America, who live and breathe Chevys, especially the sought-after, innovative for the times '55 to '57 Tri-Chevys. They knew exactly where to find crucial missing bits, like tailgate windows, even if it meant ordering parts from three provinces away. All the clips holding on the miles of chrome trim on the car's front, back and sides had rusted and needed replacing. 'Two weeks, tops,' promised the local supplier, who wasn't on the Chevy brethren list but was closer than three provinces away.

While Ken did time in car-sanding purgatory I thought it only prudent to look busy. I stocked up on camping essentials: dill pickle potato chips, pillow-sized bags of marshmallows for toasting around campfires, and my mother's home-baked cinnamon buns, Saskatoon berry pies and peanut butter cookies. I sewed magnetised curtains for the car's windows. One of the Chevy brethren passed on the bright idea of making a cheesecloth anti-mosquito 'sleeve'. Open door, slip sleeve over door, close door, roll down window. Ingenious. Ken whipped up a piece of screen to clip on in front of the radiator to keep the notorious prairie insects from clogging it up. He attached a compass to the windshield, to keep my notorious navigating from landing us in Mexico.

My family spun wild beast stories to prepare us for a return to life in the Canadian mammalian world after years of life in the New Zealand bird world. This was the year of bad bears. A grizzly bear dragged down and killed a woman hiker hiding in a tree in Alberta. A mother grizzly nipped a camper's buttocks in Banff National Park. Black bears got into the act, too: one peeled off a forestry worker's scalp like a hat and chewed on her legs in British Columbia; another gnawed a bush pilot to pieces in the Northwest Territories. A cougar had been spotted prowling around my nieces' primary school. The principal cautioned them against approaching very large kitties.

This was too much nature for my liking. Maybe we needed to pack something more lethal than a pillow-sized bag of marshmallows.

Over the weeks things fell into place. Ken scoured rust, painted, sanded, painted, sanded, until, with help from patient panel-beater relatives, the Beast glowed a sexy copper and cream. If we ignored the bullet-sized holes along the sides and back where the chrome clips and chrome trim should be, Beast was now quite a Beauty.

Five weeks after placing the order the chrome clips arrived from the Saskatoon supplier. They were exactly the wrong thing. The choices were clear: either start our road trip in a 'Bonnie and Clyde died here' car, or smother each other with the marshmallows and end it all.

I ordered more chrome clips from a Chevy brethren-approved supplier who knew the letters of the alphabet and could count to ten.

We stuffed the car to the headliner with mattresses, pillows, duvets, bug shirts, mosquito nets, torches, crockery, cutlery, food bins, our trusty Trangia alcohol stove, maps of every province and major city, a casket-sized tool box and almost as large socket set, and Mom's muffins, pasta sauce, ham soup and a large luxurious fruitcake.

'We're going on a road trip, not to jail,' said Ken, who'd been pared down to an unhealthy boniness by sheer Beastliness.

While we packed, Mom, for whom food is love, shared a tin of chocolate chip cookies and her Essential Rules of Travel:

Rule 1: Always put your canned food in a covered bin so when you have to brake hard you won't be knocked unconscious by a flying can of beans.

Rule 2: Remember to say hello to everyone you meet in small towns. Otherwise they'll think you're stuck up.

Rule 3: If you run out of warm clothing go to a lost-and-found and claim something cosy, maybe a nice thick woolly sweater.

A neighbour from across the street moseyed over for a nosey. 'Say, is that a '57 Chevy? I had a '57 Ford wagon once. One time we went camping and there was a storm, so me, the wife, her folks and our three kiddies all slept in the wagon.'

'It's a '56 Chevy,' I said with authority.

Ken turned the key. The Beast started like a rocket. Time to put rubber on the road. If four adults and three children could sleep in a classic wagon, so could we.

Gas, Gobble and Go

' It's a big egg, fer sure. '

Giant-egg fan, Vegreville, Alberta

On our way, at last. Then a nostalgic urge to revisit some fondly remembered Saskatchewan places before moving on to pastures new took root. 'Let's go to Wanuskewin. Here's the turn-off.'

'What? I've only been driving for a minute.'

'I like Wanuskewin.'

'I'm not watching any dancing.' Ken rates watching dance performances somewhere between movies about relationships and opera singing on his list of Things to Avoid Like the Plague.

'Let's make a deal. I get Wanuskewin. You get that car show in Prince Albert, when we visit your parents.'

'Done.'

Wanuskewin means 'living in harmony' in the language of the Cree First Nation, whose natural heritage park this is. We spent a harmonious hour roaming trails along the river under a prairie sky falling clear down to our feet, sage and sunburnt grasses sweet on the breeze. I liked the hoary old stones the buffalo, in the days when they ran in meaty rivers across the plains, leaned up against for a good old scratch. Ken liked the cunningly constructed tipis.

'We could take one of these camping.'

'We have a tent,' I reminded him. 'We drive it.'

Then: 'Today Roberta is performing the circle dance,' bellowed a man with a microphone. 'It's a women's dance. Roberta is wearing forty pounds of beads, so it's a slow dance.'

'Let's go,' said Ken.

'We can't just leave. It's rude. We're already sitting here.'

Breathtakingly beaded and boned, feathered and fringed, Roberta danced in a slow, mesmerising rhythm. Up on tiptoe, down, step. Up on tiptoe, down, step. Her deerskin fringe swished like prairie grass in the wind.

'Now everyone join in. Come on, everyone stand up and hold hands.'

Low moan from Ken.

I poked him. 'It'll be over soon.'

It wasn't. For several self-conscious minutes a bunch of strangers held each other's sweaty hands in a slow circle shuffle.

'You owe me two car shows,' said Ken later in the Chevy. I had to agree.

To get over the shame of dancing, Ken amused himself with his new, improved Chevy toy. He took the keys out of the car's ignition as we drove along. He honked the newly boosted trumpet horns at every living and dead thing.

'What are you honking at?'

'That gopher.'

'It's dead. It can't hear you.'

The dead outnumbered the living. Two disembowelled porcupines (too slow to live) lay squished on the road and a dead deer (too witless) in the ditch. 'Go slow and save a little doe,' read a sign advertising car insurance. Gophers played gopher chicken with the two-ton Chevy and every other wheeled thing on the highway. If a gopher didn't make it to the other side another one ran out and nibbled the crushed remains. Then the nibbling gopher got run down and another cannibal gopher scooted out to try its luck. And so on in the mysterious way of gophers, whose other goal in life is to dig holes large enough for folks to trip in, fall flat on their face and rip a hole in their trousers.

The new-look Beast redeemed its hideous faults with many original features. The long curved windows framed a panorama of all there was to view: whipped-cream clouds floating in an upside-down bowl of blue; fields of canola so eye-smackingly yellow if you looked up 'yellow' in the dictionary it would say, 'Go see a Saskatchewan canola field.' The car had room enough for all our possessions in the back and us in the front, as well as a small stowaway or some contraband in the well in front of the engine.

The trademark chrome Chevrolet 'bird' on the bonnet pointed the way. (Something had to. The compass settled on NE and never moved again.) The twin-humped padded dashboard mirroring the twin curves of the fenders made me feel a little, although not that much, better about wearing lap belts: if the Beast hit something larger than a gopher, a centimetre of ancient foam stood between tooth, bone and metal.

One of the Chevy's cleverest inventions was the vent windows. Hand cranked to the perfect angle to deflect a flow of fresh air across sweaty faces, these little windows outperformed the cold, stale air conditioning of modern cars in every way but one. As we departed Wanuskewin a butterfly smacked into the vent cocked out like an elbow on my side, bounced across the car in a flawless trajectory and splattered its small but juicy guts on Ken's cheek.

'Ehhch! I've got bug guts on my face! Can you turn that window so they don't come in?'

'Then it's too hot,' I complained, handing him a tissue and searching for the mangled corpse. 'You turn your window my way, and I'll turn mine.'

'No.'

'Bug guts on you then.'

'Smuts 1' read the sign.

Bug guts and dancing forgotten, we bumped down a gravel road to Smuts. There was not a soul around. A strip of wheezy shop fronts sagged at the knees and at the lone house across the road not a curtain twitched, nor a dog barked or chicken scratched. It was as if the town folk had gone for a collective community stroll and forgotten how to get back.

This lack of citizenry made the town's not one, but two dazzling Ukrainian Orthodox churches all the more mysterious. Their onion-shaped domes – although no onion was ever this shapely – shone silver-bright against a sky so saturated with blue it nearly dripped from the heavens. I rattled a doorknob in a 'break, enter and steal the collection plate' sort of way, but still no one appeared.

The Ukrainian church reminded me of my mission to see some of Canada's Giant Roadside Things. Many countries have Giant Roadside Things. Some are more thrilling than others. In Australia and New Zealand they're often fruit (the big pineapple) or vegetables (the big carrot). Canada favours giant mammals and birds, and the products thereof. First on the list was the giant Ukrainian easter egg of Vegreville, next door in Alberta.

Back on the road bevies of butterflies and a crop of bumble bees kamikazed into the vent windows and the radiator anti-bug screen. Whenever we stopped, Ken unclipped the screen and shook out a battlefield's worth of these innocent victims. Plus hordes of wasps, unmourned.

'Let's go to Batoche,' I said. 'Here's the turn-off.'

'What! We're never going to get anywhere if you want to stop every ten minutes.'

'This *is* anywhere. I like Batoche. You do too. There's no dancing. I promise.'

And so another peaceful hour passed among the trembling aspen and Saskatoon berry bushes, in the still prairie air, wandering the rifle pits of Batoche where the Métis people – part Cree, part French Canadian – lost their last stand against Canadian militia not much more than a hundred years before. Rebel leader Louis Riel was hanged for treason. Hanged! That part of school history always gave me the shivers.

In Prince Albert, Ken got to see the car show. Even better, he got to be *in* the car show.

'I was looking for a parking spot. The guy said, "Are you in the show?" I said "No." He said, "Why not? It's free."' Ken likes a good bargain.

'What did people say about the Beast?'

'Nice car, too bad it's missing all the chrome.'

My in-laws plied us with plenty of warmth, food and drink, and sent us on our way with even less room in the Chevy.

The prairies soon gave way to scraggle-headed jack pines and the insect world fell behind. A couple of coyotes discussing strategy in the ditch flicked us the insolent coyote eye. Coyotes are sheep slaughterers and chicken thieves. Farmers despise them and there would be no giant coyotes to see along the roadside. But I liked their sharp-eyed wily look and silvery-russet coats. As a city kid visiting my grandparents' Moon Lake farm near Saskatoon I'd often heard coyotes howling on hillsides in the moonlight and staunchly believed, no matter what country folk claimed, that the coyotes were serenading the moon, not rallying for a raid on Grandma's hens.

These coyotes needed to watch their step; this was hunting and fishing country. We barrelled through the pines to Spiritwood, population 999, and pulled up outside the Spiritwood Café. Formica tables, vinyl bench seats polished to a gloss by past and present bottoms, pumpkin, cherry, chocolate cream pie on the menu; this was the best kind of diner. The stuffed deer heads nailed to the wall reproached customers for even thinking about burgers. Instead I ordered newborn potatoes to be brutishly slaughtered for French fries.

'You want just fries, or poutine?'

Poutine? I looked at the waitress, and at the glum deer head hovering above her. If either of them knew what poutine was, they weren't saying. The waitress poked her pen at the blackboard. 'French fries $3, Poutine $4.'

'It costs another loonie.'

In our absence from the country, Canada's one-dollar notes had vanished. Loonies had appeared in their place. On one side of the coin there was Her Majesty the Eternal Monarch, on the other Canada's bird darling, the loon. The duck-like loon croons a lament so eerie, so hair-raisingly keening it deserves to have a gold coin if not something grander, like a car, named after it. (The two-dollar coins featuring a polar bear on the back are called, for some reason, toonies not bearies.)

Anything costing a whole loonie more had to be extra good. We ordered it, and it was. Trowelled thick as plaster on crisp fat fries, the cheese curds and dark brown beef gravy melted gooily together and dripped down amongst the crevices. We licked poutine sauce off lips and felt pulses for signs of stiffening arteries. I thought about ordering some for the road in case we needed to gum up a leak somewhere.

Outside Spiritwood a freshly dead coyote sprawled across the centre line, its plush fur matted with blood. Run down, not gunned down.

'That's one flat coyote,' said Ken. He guided the Beast around the fallen one, so as not to flatten it further.

All the town's chickens stood up and hurrahed, but it was an unhappy thing, a flat coyote of a thing to happen. From then on, all dismal events, should there be any, would be flat coyotes.

To cheer myself up I lobbied long and hard for a stopover at the Hafford Polkafest.

'No more dancing,' said Ken firmly. 'And, if you hadn't noticed, we're still in Saskatchewan.'

'Okay. We're leaving now.'

Onwards to Alberta and the world's largest Ukrainian easter egg. If Canada's other Giant Roadside Things turned out to be half as impressive as the giant egg, this would be a memorable trip. Crafted of shining bronze, silver and gold aluminium, and patterned in exquisite triangular shapes the ten-metre oval was the ultimate in egg art. According to the brochure, it represented the first computer modelling of an egg. It was also a clever egg, acting as a weather vane in the wind while coddling gently in the sunshine. It thrilled me to my inner yolk. I wasn't the only one so moved. The egg-gazer standing next to me whipped out his cellphone.

'Guess where I am, man – I'm outside Vegreville looking at the giant egg. Man it's big. Yeah, it's a big egg, fer sure.'

It was for sure a big egg, a beautiful egg. The only thing more marvellous than this egg would be the mysterious giant chook that laid it. I was glad we'd stopped, even if dusk was falling and campsites seemed a little thin on the ground. I voted for driving on to Edmonton for a good night's rest in an igloo-shaped bed at a posh hotel at another Giant Roadside Thing, the West Edmonton Mall. Ken argued for staying true to course and camping. Nature won.

At Elk Island National Park, though, nature didn't come cheap.

'You'll need a day pass for the park.' The ranger peered at us from the safety of the park office booth. 'That's twelve dollars.'

'It's seven-thirty at night,' Ken pointed out. 'There's not much of the day left.'

'Sorry sir, it's the rules. It's another twenty-three dollars for camping—'

'Twenty-three dollars!'

'—and five dollars for firewood. There's an extra charge for a wilderness permit if you're doing any hiking and camping in the back country of a national park. Say, is that a '57 Chevy? I had a '58 Ford pick-up once.'

'It's a '56 Chevy.' I handed forty dollars across the fuming Ken, who I could tell was gearing up to demand 'And how much does air cost?'

'There ya go. Take good care of that car.'

'Thanks. Will do.' I stuck the park pass on the window.

'Bastards,' said Ken.

There was no extra charge for watching a beaver beavering around its log lodge or a placid porcupine nibbling clover near the shower block. Squirrels dashed about doing burglar assaults on picnic tables and nipping the hands that didn't feed them. A squirrel nip, though, wasn't to be taken lightly. Signs posted around the park warned of a tick-borne rabbit fever disease in the area. Symptoms sounded evil: skin ulcers, fever and chills, swollen spleen and, for the really unlucky, fatal pneumonia. The warnings only mentioned rabbits and mustelids, so as along as we weren't dancing with badgers it was probably safe. I stepped away from the sign, tripped in a gopher hole, fell flat on my face and ripped my trousers.

Driving an old gas-sucking V8 Chevy was not the cheapest way to travel the country, as friends, acquaintances and total strangers pointed out. Our petrol budget equalled a down payment on a modest house in a modest prairie town or, in somewhere like Smuts, possibly a whole town. Alberta, though, oozed oil and gas from under every rock and out of every bog. Petrol prices were the lowest in the land.

At a petrol station near Jarvis a silent old chap in a crisp white shirt, suspenders and a chronically surprised smile rang up the tankful of petrol and a pack of bison salami. The till declared the total to be $42,679.10.

'I don't think that's quite right,' I pointed out.

He tried again. It totalled $3010.29. His benevolent grin never wavered.

'Better try once more,' I suggested.

Finally we arrived at the digestible amount of $43.57.

He burst into garrulousness. 'Say, is that a '57 Chevy? I had a '55 Chevy two-door once.'

Past Flatbush, lines of toothpick pines marched endlessly on. How could there be so many? Pines are fine in moderation. They provide a home for many forest creatures. They smell nice and piny. But after a few hours they get in the way of the view. I wanted them gone.

The town of Slave Lake offered a glimpse of a choppy grey lake and a chance for a little chortle with the locals at the next petrol station. The Chevy's best-kept secret was how to fill the petrol tank. Nozzle in hand, the teenage attendant wandered round and round the car. 'Where do I put this?'

A clutch of leathery old fellows standing around chewing toothpicks chuckled. 'This here's a '56 Chevy, sonny,' said one. 'Show 'em how it works. You ain't seen nothin' like it.'

Ken showed them. He twisted a lever on top of the left tail light. The entire tail light opened downwards away from the car. Inside was the secret petrol cap.

'It's darn near the best thing General Motors ever come up with.'

We also stocked up on Pepsi, two cases at $6.99 each. The total came to almost $24.

'What happened to the fourteen bucks for two cases?'

'There's the GST, and the environmental tax and the deposit to pay on the cans,' apologised the checkout lady. 'People forget about the taxes. It all adds up.'

'Bastards,' said Ken.

Nearer the British Columbia border, High Prairie, a sweet neat town with treed streets and groomed lawns, looked like a good bet for camping. The friendly woman in the tourist office pointed the way to a deserted grassy plot beside the baseball diamond lacking facilities other than a warped picnic table and probably a resident ghoul. Heavy-duty earthmoving machinery rumbled all around the only other option at the south end of town, but at least it showed signs of life.

A couple in the next campsite invited us to their camper for happy hour.

'Did your car come from one of the car graveyards near Saskatoon?' asked Eileen.

'No, but it was nearly dead when we got it,' said Ken.

Gordon and Eileen were visiting Eileen's relatives. As one of fifteen children in a Métis family, Eileen had quite a few to visit. In his seventies, Eileen's father, like Louis Riel before him, had taken up the fight for Métis rights. Oil companies running pipes through Métis land were supposed to compensate the owners, but no money ever came their way. He fought the oil companies in court for ten years. He won.

'But a lot of our people weren't happy. He said, I'm not giving the money to them. I'm putting it in a trust for the children's education. Then he told the government, don't send people to build the houses, send someone to supervise so we can build them ourselves.'

Eileen was her father's daughter. 'I could apply for treaty rights – I could get free medical and dental and some free schooling – but I don't need it. People appreciate things more if they work for it.'

This was a place of movers and shakers. Outside High Prairie a sign showing a map of the western provinces declared, 'Independence is the only way' and listed a phone number for western rebels to call. French Québec periodically lurched towards a split from Canada, but the western provinces were not happy with their lot either. As far as many prairie folk I'd talked to were concerned, all Ottawa politicians were shiftless no-account liars and thieves. The west was better off riding into the sunset alone, though so far it hadn't happened. That hadn't stopped the jangling of separatist spurs, at least around High Prairie. As we left the town a country singer longed for 'Fast cars and freedom' on the radio.

I directed Ken past Sturgeon Heights and Crooked Creek to Clairmont in search of Kelly's Bar. Here, promised my guidebook, bar patrons sat on stools made of saddles and drank shooters served in bull-semen specimen tubes. A more western experience one could not hope for. But Kelly's Bar failed to appear: inside the only vaguely bar-like building in town a disco ball dangled and video machines jangled. There were no saddle stools and not a soul in the place.

'This hasn't been Kelly's Bar for at least eight years,' reckoned the barmaid.

'That guidebook's not worth its weight in cow shit,' said Ken.

As a consolation prize I persuaded him to stop at the town of Beaverlodge to view the giant concrete beaver. A sign posted outside the beaver enclosure advised visitors to enter at their own risk.

'Why, is it a killer beaver?' asked Ken, who likes a challenge.

More likely this version of Canada's national rodent had a bad case of rabbit fever disease. Big, brown and buck-toothed, the unfortunate beaver was not a patch on the exquisite egg of Vegreville.

Over the border in British Columbia the price of petrol jumped twenty cents per litre.

'Bastards,' said Ken.

Yukon or Bust

' The price of fur was good that year. '

*Marl Brown, beard donor, Fort Nelson,
British Columbia*

At Dawson Creek a sign at one of western Canada's few roundabouts announced, 'You are now entering the World Famous Alaska Highway.' Well, almost. The navigator missed the exit and the driver had to go round again like a gormless tourist who'd never seen a roundabout before. This time the driver nailed Mile Zero, the start of a world famous road.

The Alaska Highway was one of those great historic feats of engineering that made modern road projects seem puny and pussy-footy, if the already suspect guidebook was to be believed. The bombing of Pearl Harbor caught the US military with its pants not just down but still hanging in the wardrobe. The Americans figured that Alaska, a short plane ride across the Bering Sea from Japan, was next on the hit list so they'd better rustle up some supply roads pronto. Thousands of unlucky American soldiers aided by just as unlucky Canadian civilian engineers crashed the road through snow and goopy muck and trees thick as quills on a porcupine. They took pot shots at hungry wildlife and slept outside in weather only a polar bear could love. Eight months and 2451 kilometres later the two ends of the Alaska–Canada military highway met in the middle and the road opened for business. So wretched was the gravelled, twisty mess that early embittered motorists cursed it as the 'junkyard of the American automobile'. That didn't scare us. Extravagantly paved since those bad old days, the highway curved down through the flat-topped Peace River Valley. Roadside pubs of the Jackfish Dundee and Cowboy Saloon ilk lured passers-by, but after the Kelly's Bar deception I was not to be lured lightly. A gun-totin' stuffed fish on a wall did not appeal. I wanted to see a moose.

When nature handed out Bambi-eyed good looks in the deer world, moose were off somewhere slurping up swamp grass.

They're hump-necked and big-nosed and have a reputation for dimwittedness. Rutting bull moose challenge freight trains to duels they can never win. Up here moose-spotting had to be a done deal – every few kilometres road signs urged, 'Caution: moose on highway'. Camera at the ready I sat back and waited for a moose or two – preferably a bull moose with an antler rack as wide as a wall – to amble alongside, knock on the window and pose for a photo.

Many hours later, still not a hint of a moose. As evening drew on, the daily search began for that just as elusive prey, a small cosy campground, one with running water, a fragrant forest amongst which to fossick for free firewood and an on-site shop well provisioned with such camping essentials as cold beer and fur hats. One just like Pink Mountain. Mile 140 on the Alaska Highway, run by a couple of nice folk named Korey and Lory.

'Why is the campground called Pink Mountain?' I asked Korey.

'Mountain out the back's pink.' He jerked his chin towards a grey shape looming behind the shop.

'Oh. Any moose in these parts?'

He pointed to a back room. 'Take a look in there.'

In there was a bull moose, or at least the head of one. The antler rack stretched as wide as the wall. I hoped it wasn't the last bull moose with wall-sized antlers ever seen in Pink Mountain.

Out front a gnarly old guy roosted on the shop's wooden stoop. His hound, a low-bellied growler, had ankle snapping on its mind.

I tried again. 'Any moose in these parts?'

'Plenty, surprised you ain't seen any. You wanna watch out fer them moose. Small car hits a moose, the legs're so high they go right through the windshield. Don't want no 1500-pound moose sittin' in yer lap kickin' you to death tryin' to get out.'

The hound dog curled a meaningful lip.

The next morning while I peered into the bushes for moose the Northern Rocky Mountains shouldered closer, sharp-shanked and gunmetal blue, rising up in the west. Past Polka Dot Creek and Buckinghorse River the road wound around the foothills; at a bend near Prophet River, unlucky Mile 217, a family of six huddled by the side of the road while rescue workers moved through the rolled-over and smashed-to-bits wreckage of what had been the family RV. There were no signs of any moose-vehicle collision.

There were, I noticed, two types of tourists on the Alaska Highway. The first drove RVs the size of a small Pacific island, each towing a marginally shorter vehicle, maybe a Hummer, and with a pair of bicycles, a couple of kayaks and always a satellite TV dish on top. The second type of tourist rode whacking great Harley-Davidson or Honda Goldwing or BMW motorcycles from North Carolina or Ontario or Kansas that poured drinks and played all your favourite classic hits and folded out into king-sized beds. Not true. They towed colour-coordinated pop-up trailers that folded out into king-sized beds.

Few of these travellers were younger than sixty. On the Alaska Highway the retirees of North America were kings of the road. They were likeable down-to-earth folk who deserved credit for having the stamina to put their backs and hips through months or even years of driving back and forth across the continent.

My own parents and siblings travelled the Alaska Highway in the summer of 1976 in a rented Winnebago. I did not accompany them. I spent the summer taking films out of mail-order envelopes and sticking them in other envelopes at a photo shop by day, and selling popcorn at a movie theatre by night. All that loot paid for my first overseas trip the next summer. Memories of that 'Round twenty countries in ten minutes' bus tour are vague. What springs to mind are Austrian flugelhorners flugelhorning their audience to a stupor, projectile vomiting in Rome after a nasty batch of pasta or was it the wine, and the tour guide seducing all the Australian women on the bus. Among the highlights of my family's Alaskan Highway adventure, I was told, were bear-spotting, a view of the country's highest mountain, Mt Logan, and a spectacular crash into the ditch when a fatigued Californian sideswiped the Winnebago. Hard to know who'd had the better trip.

So far, on this leg of our journey, crashes were thicker on the ground than moose.

Ken remained optimistic. 'Got your moose lens on the

camera?'

'Nope. I took it off. There are no moose. It's a local joke on tourists. Like the sasquatch.'

'You'll be sorry.'

Not a minute later, I was. Something thrashed violently in the roadside grass. A cow and calf moose broke through. Ken braked hard. The cow moose gazed at the car, dismissed it as yet another noxious object in a near-sighted moose's challenging world, and clambered onto the highway a few hundred metres ahead. Mama moose and child gangled across the road, crick-legged, bulb-snouted, utterly lovely. So excited was I, the moose lens didn't get a look in. It was a moose moment, a very happy thing. Flat coyotes bad; moose moments good.

On a moose-induced high we floated into the small forestry, oil and gas town of Fort Nelson. Once a rough 'n' ready fur-trading frontier town, Fort Nelson, Mile 300, now boasted the world's largest disposable chopstick factory – or so claimed the guidebook. Two billion pairs per year rolled out the doors. It was turning into a day of highlights.

The helpful young woman at the visitor information centre apologised. 'The factory's been closed for a couple of years,' she reckoned. 'But we do have a good museum.' The Fort Nelson Historical Museum may or may not have been as intriguing as a disposable chopstick factory – I will never know – but it had many fine and carefully tended attractions, among them stuffed lynx and other lifelike forest creatures, a shed full of lovingly restored Studebakers and Dodges, exceptional black-and-white film footage of Alaska Highway workers slogging through snow and even a genuine piece of the equipment that built it, a cable-operated hoe.

The museum's sumptuously bearded founder and curator wandered out for a look at the Beast.

'Have you lived here long?'

'Yep, for about a hundred years.'

Marl Brown wasn't quite that old, but his beard looked like it might have been. Marl once sacrificed his trademark Rip van Winkle-style whiskers for the museum's cause. The Get the Beard

Off contingent, so the story goes, outbid the Friends of the Beard at a fund-raising dinner, 'so one of the ladies whipped out a pair of manicure scissors and chopped it off on the spot. It looked like the rats had been at it. That was 1982. The beard hasn't been cut since, apart from the odd bit of self-trimming. I catch it on fire now and again.'

The beard sold for ten thousand dollars. That, I marvelled, was probably the world's most expensive beard.

'The price of fur was good that year,' said Marl.

The Yukon border lay more than five hundred kilometres and only a smattering of petrol stations ahead. The road north from Fort Nelson climbed, climbed, climbed out of oil-soaked muskeg up the Rockies' granite flanks. At a splendid hilly viewpoint past the hamlet of Steamboat, Ken squinted at something beneath the Beast.

'Is that our puddle or someone else's puddle?'

He got onto his hands and knees and peered under the car. He came up rubbing something greasy between his fingers.

'Transmission fluid,' he said. 'Feck.'

The junkyard of the American automobile had crippled another victim. The Beast had failed its first seriously hilly test since leaving the flat-as-a checkerboard prairies. To be fair, Steamboat Mountain was the steepest part of the Alaska Highway, but we'd expected the 'rebuilt transmission' to go the distance, not just to Mile 333. The breakdown rated at least two very, very flat coyotes.

The transmission still shifted from park to drive to reverse, but for how long, who could say. Prospects did not look good: keep going north and risk a right good stranding eight hours from any hope of help if the transmission failed completely, or turn back to Fort Nelson and cross fingers the local garage could do a quick, cheap fix-it job.

Back down the hill at Steamboat, Ken looked under the bonnet the way you do if you're a car owner pondering a problem and there are other car owners around also wanting to look under the bonnet and ponder the problem. I bought two litres of transmission fluid from the suspiciously well-stocked café.

'You're not the first to blow a gasket up here,' said the woman behind the counter.

Maybe not, but I was willing to bet the price of a new transmission that ours was the first '56 Chevrolet in many a decade to fall foul of Steamboat Mountain. We crept back to Fort Nelson, stopping every fifteen minutes to check if the leak had gushed into a fountain. The local mechanics poked and frowned and quoted an eye-watering sum to fix the problem. Nope it wouldn't be any time soon. Parts for Chevys weren't just lying around on the ground. Not even a good glop of poutine could fix that leak.

We parked the disgraced Beast in a Fort Nelson campground and considered the options. Fix the car here at painful cost and lose travelling time. Try for a bigger town with cheaper, faster mechanics back down the highway. Sell the miserable thing to Marl for a pittance and take a bus across the rest of the country.

It was hard to know how serious the problem might be. On the European trip the Ford van completely conked out in a campground near Florence. Furious, fed up and ready to abandon the car to life as a campground ornament, Ken started packing up our belongings while I sprinted off to find out when the next train left for Rome. By the time I returned the Ford had thought better of such shenanigans and started up sweet as you please. The Chevy's problem might be just as transient.

Ken phoned Bruce for a bit of mechanic's advice.

'Don't put one cent into rebuilding that transmission,' warned Bruce. 'Stop Leak might work, you could try it. But it might not. The whole thing could seize.'

Ken sunk into a deep, dark, despairing bog. After all his hard slog, to break down three days into a three-month trip was almost more than a mortal could bear. This was seriously worrying – my beloved is irrepressibly and often unjustifiably cheerful in the jaws of disaster. I felt an urge to run around in circles howling like a coyote, a strategy always helpful in times of crisis. But I didn't want to spook the RV owners, in case we needed to beg a lift from one of them.

One couple, a lady horse-whisperer and her husband, invited us into their home on wheels for a consoling wine and cupcakes. But she didn't hold much hope for our chances of getting a lift.

'You could ask someone for a ride, but most RVs aren't set up for more than a couple of people.'

A bottle or so of red wine and many anguished hours later we struck on another plan. Leave the wretched car somewhere in Fort Nelson – good luck to anyone who tried to steal it – and take a northbound bus the next day to the Yukon's capital city of Whitehorse, where family friends had offered to show us a bit of the place. To do the trip by bus, not Beast, was more spirit-crushing than missing out on the disposable chopstick factory. But at least we'd get to see the Yukon, if not by shiftless Chevrolet.

We could think of only one person in Fort Nelson who might store the car. In the morning Marl, bless him and his lovely beard, stopped retooling a tractor part and offered space in his private shed. With barely a backward glance we abandoned the Beast to repent its sins amongst Marl's three-wheeled inventions and waiting-to-be-restored Fords.

At the Greyhound bus depot the ticket seller also took pity. She sold us the cheapest tickets she could squeeze from the system.

'Come back at around three o'clock. The bus is a little late, and could be fairly full.'

'What happens if there are too many people for the bus?'

'We strap 'em to the front bumper.' She handed me the tickets. 'Be here on time.'

There was no need to prepare for life as bus bumpers; only a dozen people got on the bus, including a retired New Zealand beef farmer from Invercargill en route to visit the brother he hadn't seen for twenty-five years. A young First Nations woman on her way back to a northern reservation tucked blankets and pillows around her heavily pregnant belly.

'You've done this before.'

'Yeah, I've got a four-year-old daughter.'

'Sorry. I meant the bus ride.'

'Lotsa times. You get used to it. They play movies the whole way up.'

We settled into the prime wildlife-spotting front seats. (Later a savvy bus traveller told me, 'Never sit in the front seats. If the bus crashes into something you'll do a human cannonball act right through the windshield.' I wondered whether he knew my mother.)

I felt perfectly safe with driver Joe. This is not always the way with bus drivers. A drunken driver in Crete nearly wiped out an entire load of shrieking passengers, us included, on a tight cliff-top bend fully occupied by a donkey cart and a scooter. Two wheels skimmed the cliff edge and only the frenzied clacking of worry-beads kept the other two on the road.

Joe was neither drunk nor Cretan. He was the chatty sort who stuck to his side of the centre line and stopped often for rest and photo breaks.

'Want to see some stone sheep, folks?'

Or a fox, or a hare. Or a dark shape in the ditch that turned out to be a black bear munching something in the long grass.

'Wonder what he's eating.'

'Probably a stranded Chevy owner,' said Ken, who hadn't quite recovered his equanimity.

The bus stopped for dinner at Toad River, Mile 422. While we waited for burgers and fries a fellow passenger, an oil rigger in snakeskin boots, offered all takers a marijuana toke behind some bushes. The oilman smoked for medicinal purposes, aided by Canadian government contractors who grew the legal pot in an abandoned copper and zinc mine shaft in remote Flin Flon, Manitoba, amidst much kerfuffle over the product's poor quality.

The oil rigger had a novel idea for fixing this problem. 'The scientists messed it up. What do they know about growing weed? They ought to give the job to the guys in jail busted for growing it – they know what to do.'

A short way down the road a herd of hefty bison grazed the roadside grass. A male swathed in a thick fur mantle stamped its hooves in an ancient dustbowl dance. It was thrilling. I'd only ever seen the domestic bison-raised-for-burgers variety, never a wild one. This was another fine moose moment.

Joe stopped for photos but warned against getting off the bus and annoying the foot-stomping alpha male. 'It's not so bad now, but in the winter the bison come down to lick the salt off the roads.

Then they lie down in the middle of the road, where it's nice and warm. The snow settles on them, then a car hits them. It's a big mess for the car, and the bison too.'

Mile 613, Watson Lake. We hopped off the bus and sprinted down the highway to the world famous signpost forest. Homesick American soldier and Alaska highway grunt Carl K. Lindley nailed up the first sign pointing to his home town of Danville, Illinois, in 1942, starting a trend for travellers to lug along signs and post them on a forest of poles. They made entertaining reading. Clamtown, PA. Quitman, TX. Hi-De-Ho Trailer Club. Köln from the German autobahn, even Dunedin, New Zealand, 14,616 kilometres. There were enough bits of the world to wander through for hours, but the bus waited for no one.

The retired Invercargill beef farmer got off the bus at Watson Lake. His long-lost brother was waiting. They shook hands.

'Go on, give him a hug,' urged Joe. 'You haven't seen each other in twenty-five years.'

'We're not the hugging kind,' said the brother sternly, and they creaked off into the dusk.

Joe, too, finished his shift at Watson Lake. The entire bus murmured regrets. The new driver put pedal to the metal, cranked up the air conditioning and blasted through the night.

There are many things to like about travelling by Greyhound bus. Passengers don't have to navigate or worry about crashing a classic car into a snoozing bison. With a bit of luck, a jovial tour guide like Joe drives the route. There is more to see from a bus than a plane window. Other passengers come and go with ordinary but interesting purpose. Things not so likeable are thirteen hours cramped up in a non-reclinable seat, having only fifteen minutes to speed read the Watson Lake signpost forest and arriving in any town, anywhere, at four-thirty in the morning.

We fell out of the bus at Whitehorse. Mile 887 and the end of the Alaska Highway for us. Family friend Marge waited in the ridiculously bright early-morning light to whisk us away in her black low-gliding Lincoln Continental. Gold nugget rings flashed on every finger. Welcome to the True North.

Tale Spinners

' Don't be afraid – come on in. '

Sign on the Snake Pit bar, Dawson City, Yukon

The Yukon Territory had sunk long claws into my imagination ever since I'd read Robert Service's ballad 'The Cremation of Sam McGee':

> There are strange things done in the midnight sun
> By the men who moil for gold;
> The arctic trails have their secret tales
> That would make your blood run cold;
> The Northern Lights have seen queer sights,
> But the queerest they ever did see
> Was that night on the marge of Lake Lebarge
> I cremated Sam McGee.

Secret tales, midnight sun, moiling for gold, arctic trails, lakeside cremations – irresistible. The Yukon had long been a place people ran away to, running from something or someone, maybe themselves, or else hunting something exciting like moose or precious metals. Their tales, some secret, some not, wove the Yukon into a whole.

In that generous way of Canadians everywhere who thought nothing of driving vast distances to buy a doughnut or entertain almost complete strangers, Marge and husband Cameron offered us a lift for the five hundred kilometres from Whitehorse to the old gold-mining town of Dawson City. The lively Marge regaled us with tales of the car accidents she'd had on these roads over the years.

'Once I rolled the truck with the acetylene tanks in the back. Another time I shot off the road so far into the woods you couldn't even see the car from the road.'

Ken, trapped in the back of the two-door Lincoln, fell asleep in alarmed self-defence.

Like so many folk trekking the mining trail the couple had prospected a claim near Keno City, close to Dawson City, but, said Cameron, 'there was no money in it'. There was, though, a decent living to be had running a café at Dawson City airport even though 'it was minus fifty to sixty degrees in the winter and bears walked by the café – I had to tell the kids to be careful,' said Marge, as casually as if talking about telling the tots to put their mittens on. 'Then the café burnt down and we escaped with only the clothes on our backs.'

The Lincoln idled into Penny's Place at Pelly Crossing for a roadside snack and a mandatory visit to a well-known loo. Festooned outside with moose antlers, the pastel-painted loos were papered inside with fabulous tales from magazines and newspapers, like the story of Lapis the cat who disappeared from its Denver, Colorado home and appeared months later, as if by magic, thousands of kilometres away in Whitehorse. How does a cat do that? And why? Only a cat knows.

At Pelly Crossing I met a distant relative who told of more incredible journeys. 'In the past,' said Lucy, 'people went everywhere by dog sled in winter and in summer hitched the dogs to a plough and tilled the land. The children travelled by riverboat from Pelly Crossing to a boarding school in Dawson City. The parents didn't know if the kids had arrived at school or even if they were alive until they returned down the river in spring.' Which beat a story about an intrepid Colorado cat any day.

The black Lincoln detoured off the Klondike Highway onto the Silver Trail to Keno City. On the mining town's dirt streets log cabins, some abandoned, some not, leaned this way and that. Once home to eight hundred hardy folk, in the boom town days when the nearby Elsa mine pumped out silver by the ton, Keno City could count its residents on two hands and two feet. I heard whispers that ghosts of lost souls haunted the Keno City Hotel. It was closed, so we couldn't check out the phantoms for ourselves, but car parts and rusty refrigerators haunted the weedy yards.

'Nobody throws anything out up here, it might come in handy,' said Cameron. There were, unfortunately, no suitable Chevrolet transmissions lying around on the ground.

Stuffed with Indian motorcycle signs, sombreros and empty tequila bottles, Mike Mancini's Keno City Snack Bar was chokka with things that might come in handy. An antique cash register caught my fancy.

'No,' said Ken.

'We could stuff it down the hole in the Beast where the spare tyre fits.'

'If you get a cash register,' said Ken, 'I'm going down the street to get that antique gas pump.'

Mike's parents emigrated from Italy to the nearby hamlet of No Cash, a disillusioning name for immigrants if ever there was one, where his father worked the Elsa mine. Mike had helped set up the town's mining museum, winnowing half a million dollars from the government purse for a project in a town of twenty people. He loved old things.

'I've been a pack rat since I was a kid. I've got a Pepsi can like the first Pepsi I ever drank. A lot of stuff in the snack bar is from houses being burnt down after the mine closed.'

While we waited for Mike to make pizza – what else do you order at an Italian snack bar in a Yukon silver-mining town – a bush pilot with sky-blue eyes sitting at the next table spun a survival story.

'Are you still flying?' someone asked.

'No. I've got to wait till the kids grow up. I flew my last plane into the trees. Well, my co-pilot did. We were doing sixty-five miles an hour and clipped some dead trees. That spun us around and then we ran through some live trees. Fuel was pouring down the windshield. We landed nose down in the trees, the pilot was knocked out cold. I had a gash over one eye, blood was pouring down my face. We walked an hour to a road and got some help.'

There were low whistles. 'That's some tale.'

'Yeah, there's more. I came back later with my truck to get my plane. I just got to where the plane was, I could see it in the trees. Then a moose ran out in front of me. It hit the truck and wrecked the radiator. So there's the steam coming out of the truck, and I could see my wrecked plane. I was so mad I got out my rifle and shot that moose as it's rolling down into the ditch.'

Not a joyful moose moment, then.

After dinner we cruised up Keno Hill, past tundra shrubs creeping flat under the hard-boned knees of the wind. Snow lay in dirty patches and whistling marmots – gopher cousins – burrowed under the caribou moss and clattering granite stones.

'Don't you dare,' I warned Ken, who lurked nearby with a handful of the white stuff I'd forever lost any fondness for and never had to deal with in Auckland.

'Ha ha ha,' said Ken.

I wiped snow off my nose and noticed that we and the marmots were not alone. Someone had built a chunky stone inukshuk at the top of Keno Hill. The small granite figure stood forlorn against the midnight sun rimming the mountains. It was hard to know which of its many functions the inukshuk was performing; warning of danger or helping us hunt caribou seemed long shots. More likely it was pointing the way for sunset watchers.

'The sun will rise over there in a couple of hours.' Cameron waved towards a spot a mere mountain top away from where the sun touched down and vaguely in the direction where the inukshuk was trying to catch our attention.

The next day's trip from Keno City may well have been fraught with more radiator-wrecking moose but I fell asleep on the smooth-riding Lincoln's plush upholstery and awoke to another century in Dawson City. The café latte bistros on riverside Front Street, tourist entertainment at can-can saloons and shops flogging grizzly-bear keychains had smoothed some of the raw-boned frontierism off the town, but the wooden boardwalks over dirt streets still rang to the clang of boot heels. They had done so since 1898, when gold stampeders poured into Dawson City thick as the infamous northern blackflies to sluice gold from such fabled creeks as Too Much Gold, Last Chance and Eldorado. Dawson City's gold rush ended a paltry four years after it started, when the gold petered out and fickle prospectors charged off to Alaska. The forty thousand golden-toothed prospectors or 'sourdoughs', dance-hall girls in Parisian gowns, madams like Bombay Peggy, who ran a houseful of 'sporting girls' alluringly called Silver Fox and Vancouver Lil, champagne-swilling bankers and down-and-out drunks all dribbled away when the gold ran out, leaving the couple of thousand staunch hunters, fishers, shop keepers and still some miners and down-and-outs to prop up the place.

At the Snake Pit bar in the delicately pink Westminster Hotel, est. 1898, a hand-lettered sign encouraged all comers: 'Don't be afraid – come on in.' The Snake Pit decor was Early Yukon Trapper: a birch-bark canoe hung over the bar, dead mammals gathered dust on the walls and the ornate pressed-steel ceiling could only be fully appreciated by patrons waking up on the floor after a heavy night. The Snake Pit regulars were already messily blotto or intent on becoming blotto quickly. Barnacle Bill gargled tunes at the piano, his mate slung low at the next table.

The bartender bent over the musician's mate. 'Time to take a rest from it.' Mumble. 'Well, you'll have to leave, you can't sleep here.' Mutter.

The bartender sighed. 'He's not so bad. The hardest part of the night is throwing Donna out.'

Sitting down, Donna didn't look like much trouble. Thin as a greyhound, clad in not much more than a greyhound would wear on a warm summer's night, she leaned on a one-armed man nursing a large beer. Standing up – well, standing up was the problem. She tilted a good thirty degrees from vertical. She staggered and stumbled and threw her arms around in an alarming marionette fashion. Next stop would be face down on the floor.

'Out you go, Donna.'

'Not goin'. Who's gonna make me.'

'Be a good girl now.'

She lurched cursing out the door, followed by the mumbler, into the sun. A round-faced black-haired woman in a red coat sitting next to us at the bar watched them go. 'Tch,' she said, shaking her head.

She took a sip of beer, then told us a tale of connubial bliss.

'See that picture on the wall, that's my parents. They're in the Guinness Book of Records, they were the longest-married couple in the world. My mother, she was married at thirteen. She had thirteen children.'

Joseph Henry Jarvis had married his barely teenaged bride, Annie, on 15 July 1921 at Moosehide, Yukon. They'd been joined in matrimony for seventy-nine years at the time of the record. Joe trapped and hunted until he was eighty-five and staked a place as a Snake Pit regular until he died, aged 103. Annie still carried on, aged 101. Despite appearances, being a Snake Pit regular wasn't necessarily bad for one's health.

We drank up and went off in search of Bombay Peggy's Dawson City digs, but the new owners of the heritage whorehouse had turfed out any trace of the sporting girls and turned it into a trendy B&B with nary a lout in the lounge bar. Ratty on piano and Marmot on harmonica played down and dirty blues but weren't a match for Barnacle Bill slobbering over the keys at the Snake Pit. Things livened up when Donna and her dissipated date fell through the door demanding a drink. The bartender refused, in the polite but firm way of trendy barkeeps. The twosome muttered and swayed and fell back out the door, wobbly as bow-legged cowboys in broken boot heels. Ratty and Marmot played on.

In the hills behind the tourist shops and can-can girls we found doughty Dawson City's backbone – flinty-eyed sled dogs staring down passers-by from sagging porches, moose antlers sprigged over doorways, and the log cabins and houses where such famous yarn-spinners as Sam McGee's creator Robert Service, Jack London of *White Fang* and *Call of the Wild* fame and the wildly prolific Pierre Berton had holed up at some time in their writerly lives.

At the Robert Service cabin we paid a few loonies to listen to an actor in a banker's suit and bow tie tell of how Service, born in Scotland where his Aunt Jeanie encouraged him to take long strides, so as not to wear out his soles, worked in Canada as a 'cow juice jerker' on a dairy farm and a bank clerk before making squillions not in gold but in mighty hilarious words. Anyone considering tossing a bucket of combustibles down a long drop where an old grandpa smoking a pipe might sit should listen to an actor in a banker's suit and bow tie recite 'The Three Bares' and think again.

The black Lincoln ferried us up Dawson City's Midnight

Dome, another scraped-raw mountain top, where locals held midnight parties on the longest day of the year. The Beast's many afflictions had thwarted our plan to party along with the Dawson City citizens that year, so I consoled myself with a midnight view of Klondike Valley, the blue humps of the Ogilvie Range folding onto each other in ribbons beyond the Yukon River. Another stone inukshuk pointed the way to tiny Moosehide, the village where the long-married Jarvises were hitched, and still the traditional summer camp of the local Trondek Hwechin First Nation. I'd have to visit them some other time. We'd already signed up to fly even further north to the 'stuck out on its own' aboriginal settlement of Old Crow, home to the caribou-hunting Vuntut Gwitchin, to see for ourselves how people lived in the land where the summer sun never sets.

Foraging Under the Midnight Sun

'I'm old but I'm not finish thinkin'.'

Miss Edith Josie, newspaper columnist,
Old Crow, Yukon

The plane to Old Crow, latitude 67° 39' north, skimmed over lakes of lapis blue and mine dredge tailings humped across the land, over treeless hills topped with cloud toupees. We landed on a plain barren but for starveling spruce, some aspen whispering in the wind and shrubs barely knee-high to a marmot.

Hooh! cried the crows, great black things with beady knowing eyes.

The Arctic wind blasted ice into bones. We'd crossed the Arctic Circle. The wind knew it. I knew it. I had a certificate to prove it, courtesy of Air North. Around the globe, I'd discovered, there was a disappointing lack of signage or even a pink fluorescent line in the sky marking the Arctic Circle or the Equator or the International Date Line. But this certificate, nicely done up in autumn tundra colours, made up for that.

At the Porcupine Bed and Breakfast on the shores of the Porcupine River, mysterious pairs of muddy boots lined the porch outside and a robust heater warmed the wood panelling inside, but not a soul popped up to take our money or point us to a bed.

'Do you think this is the right place? Maybe this is somebody's house.'

'Look, there's some Nutella. Let's stay here anyway.'

Ken helped himself to the Nutella on the kitchen table. I made tea. Still no one appeared, so we piled on all available clothing and ventured out onto the frank and friendly streets of Old Crow. Not five minutes into the walk a mustachioed fellow beckoned us out of the freezing breeze into the forestry office. Harvey Kassi and his shy young fellow officer Stephen Charlie fought fires, mounted search-and-rescue missions, and entertained the handful of visitors who journeyed this far up the Yukon. Some paddled for many bear- and bug-infested miles by river canoe, most flew in, and still others snowmobiled over the ice in winter. The caribou arrived under their own hoof power.

'We depend on the caribou coming north of the Dempster Highway in May for the calving, then again in September,' said Harvey. 'There must be a hundred and twenty thousand caribou in the herd – they float down the river on ice or swim.' They used everything from the caribou, he said. Meat to eat, skins for moccasins and mittens. Caribou antlers decorated sheds and posts and made an inventive fence.

I'd heard that the US government wanted to mine the Alaska Wildlife Refuge for oil, in the interests of 'national security'.

'It's a big problem. That's where the Porcupine caribou herd calves. If the caribou disappear, we can't live,' said Harvey. 'Here, try some drymeat.' He offered a bit of meat peeled off the skin. It tasted like meat-flavoured sawdust. 'We collect blueberries, raspberries, blackcurrants, salmonberries, for making jam – do you make your own jam?'

I shook my head.

'Didn't think so,' said Harvey. 'You look like the lazy type.'

'Can I speak to an elder?' I asked, to divert attention from my domestic shortcomings.

'Sure. He dialled a number and handed me the phone. 'Say, I respect you, my elder.'

'Hello. I respect you, my elder,' I said, most respectfully.

There was silence on the other end.

'I'm not an elder,' spluttered a youngish-sounding woman on the other end. 'That Harvey, he's such a joker.'

Most elders were off on a government-funded helicopter trip to their ancestral lands with a film crew to record their stories. Harvey's sister-in-law Tracy Kassi was the film-maker, Harvey said. 'She's from New Zealand.' Pull the other one.

Young Stephen took over as unofficial but enthusiastic guide. In the winter he drove dog-sled teams two hours upriver to Crow Flats to trap muskrats, mink, marten, lynx, sometimes wolverine.

'I get five dollars each for muskrat. About three hundred for lynx.' He showed off a full-length coat made of marten skins from a single night's trapping. It felt warm. I wanted it.

Across the road at the community centre a row of older men sat outside on a bench, smoking and watching Old Crow's younger men drive quad-bikes up and down the roads. Quad-bikes ruled the community's few streets. If you wanted a truck it cost ten thousand dollars to bring it by Hercules aeroplane. Plus the cost of the truck. And then where would you go?

'This is my uncle Victor.' I shook hands with a charming fellow in a battered hat like an extravagant chamber pot. Another elder strolled over to chat about fish. Next to caribou, fish rated high on the most-wanted list of foodstuffs.

'The salmon fight when you net them, they're as big as dogs. Lots of grizzlies up there, they scoop the fish out, they don't need any nets. Canoeists coming down the river carry freeze-dried food but bah, it tastes like sawdust.' Just like caribou drymeat, then.

Inside the centre, Stephen pointed to a giant wooden tongue depressor. 'Here's the board we stretch the 'rat skins on. And here's a mammoth tusk. They're lying around on the ground all around here. This clam shell is ten thousand years old.' Eager to show us where these goodies came from and where the caribou herds ran, Stephen drove us on a quad-bike up Crow Mountain. Endless, boundless vastness rolled out to the far corners of the earth. At the top of a rise the feral wind chewed ears and noses. How I wished for a lost-and-found abundant with unclaimed thick woolly sweaters or a muskrat coat.

'In caribou season this is covered with animals. As far as you can see. In the winter the caribou turn white.'

I contemplated the vision of tens of thousands of caribou thundering across the tundra, many to meet their doom on the dinner table.

In the midst of an Old Crow summer, my hands and feet were slowly freezing into ice blocks. Stephen stood in shirtsleeves and smoked a cigarette.

'Strange weather, eh. It snowed a couple of weeks ago. Two days ago it was stinking hot. In the winter it's minus fifty-five degrees and dark all the time, except for a couple of hours in the early afternoon.'

Hooh! cried the crows.

The ride back down the mountain was swift as a caribou, colder than calamity and blew the sunglasses right off Ken's face. Near the river a bunch of canoeists, bulked up in all-weather jackets and sensible hats, stood stiff as frozen mink around their boats.

'We're canoeing a thousand miles down the northern waterways,' said the tour guide. 'Is there anything interesting to see in town?'

Didn't he know? What kind of tour guide was he? The kind that seduces all the Australian women on the boats, probably. I pointed them in the direction of the warm friendly community centre and Stephen, who knew all about good guiding.

The Porcupine B&B – it *was* the right place – doubled as a base camp for incoming helicopter pilots and field researchers from outside Old Crow. That explained the line of muddy boots. A grub-smudged Baby Bear of a palaeontologist wandered in, asked who'd been eating her Nutella and wandered off with the remains. A canoeing couple poked their heads in to the cabin looking for a room. Ours, I knew, was the last available room for rent in Old Crow. I briefly considered subletting the sofa.

'How did you end up here – did you take a wrong turn?' The helicopter pilot had just come back from flying the mystery film maker Tracy Kassi around the north. I eloquently explained that, well, we just wanted to come, and set about making dinner. Forewarned that the Old Crow general store charged exorbitant prices for pretty much everything, I'd packed three bananas, four bread rolls and a can of vegetable and beef soup.

During the search for a can opener a shy young girl appeared in the doorway bearing a Styrofoam plate.

'For you,' she murmured to an archaeologist propped up at the table munching salad and eggs, and vanished.

He lifted the foil from a grilled fillet of grayling, freshly baked bannock bread and a pasta salad. It smelled like the first meal on earth. He offered the plate to the pilot. 'I'm full – do you want this?'

'Nope, I'm full too.'

The archaeologist pondered the plate. 'How about you – do you want this?'

We ditched the tin of soup and fell upon the meal, savage as grizzlies on salmon.

Archaeology around Old Crow, according to the archaeologist, went back more than twenty-five thousand years. The nearby Bluefish caves showed signs of human habitation, probably the oldest in North America. Caribou, lions, mammoths, horses and giant beavers once roamed the place. Even back then beavers were the king of rodents. These antediluvian monsters ballooned to 220 kilograms and stretched more than two metres from tooth to tail. They may have looked something like the Giant Beaver of Beaverlodge, which in light of this knowledge took on a new, interesting persona.

Another of Old Crow's interesting personae was a newspaper columnist. Miss Edith Josie started writing a monthly column for the *Whitehorse Star* in the early 1960s. Called 'Here Are the News' it chronicled daily happenings in Old Crow: 'ALBERT ABEL WENT UP RIVER SET TRAP AROUND DRIFT WOOD. HE CAME BACK. HE CAUGHT 9 MARTINS, 1 WEASEL. GEE, HE'S LUCKY MAN.' Written in Miss Edith's unique English-Gwitchin hybrid, the column was a worldwide hit. She still writes the news.

After demolishing the grayling we reswaddled and waddled off to knock on the door of Miss Edith's neat red cabin. A polished walnut of a woman invited us into the warmth, where a pot of salmon heads boiled on the stove and Led Zeppelin's 'Stairway to Heaven' blared on the radio. Miss Edith was eighty-four, although she told everybody she was eighty. 'I'm going to be this age when I'm a hundred.'

She never married, had two sons and a daughter, and brooked no sass from anybody. 'I'm old but I'm not finish thinkin'. Some people in the village want to pull down my parents' house after they die. I fly to Whitehorse to tell the people in the government, these people want to pull down my parents' house. When I get back people say to me, eh, eh, you go to Whitehorse, talk about our business. But they don't pull down my parents' house.'

She lamented the modern hustle-bustle. In the clinging warmth of the cabin, the smell of boiled salmon heads sifting into nostrils, Miss Edith's stories conjured up visions of the old ways.

'Things are different now. Now everybody so busy busy all the time. In the old days some people cut down some skinny spruce to make a canoe. My grandmother sewed a moosehide over the spruce. Then they put eight sled dogs in it and went down the river to find the caribou. Gone long time. In the old days the caribou were all over the plains, hundreds and thousands of them. Now not so many.'

On the way back we bumped into Tracy the film-maker, born in Napier to a schoolteacher father and his far-from-home Old Crow wife. Harvey the joker had told the truth.

The sun still shone a thin light through the B&B window at midnight. Ken, who would slumber through a natural disaster, said, 'There's the midnight sun, I've seen it,' and fell asleep in a trice. The helicopter pilot taped foil over his windows and did the same. I sat by the window learning Vuntut Gwitchin words from a book by the light of this spunky sun. *Vadzaih.* Caribou. *Edik'ànaantii.* Take care. *Màhsi.* Thank you.

One o'clock: went to bed. Two o'clock: thought about tying socks over eyes to keep out the light. Three o'clock. Four o'clock. Five o'clock.

Some time during that never-ending eventide I fell asleep. In the morning both the sun and I had the watery washed-out look of an otherworldly thing that's been up all night.

The B&B, it transpired, was a B only. It supplied bed. Not breakfast. The helicopter pilot had bought the last of the bread and milk from the Old Crow store, said the archaeologist. The bacon in the fridge belonged to somebody else, probably Baby Bear. The bananas and bread rolls had gone for lunch the day before. I searched for the can opener again. Vegetable and beef soup made a fine breakfast when there was nothing else but caribou drymeat.

Hooh! cried the crows.

The plane out of Old Crow landed in the Northwest Territories town of Inuvik to refuel. This is one of Canada's most northerly outposts; next stop, Greenland. Or Siberia. I glimpsed Inuvik's igloo-shaped Our Lady of Victory Roman Catholic church on the way in but couldn't spot a pub where, I'd been told, all the walls and the floor were tiled, for ease of hosing down whatever bodily juices might get splashed around during a hard night's session. We poked through the airport shop, which sold beaded moccasins at northern outpost prices, and took each other's photos beside a stuffed polar bear. The tin of soup hadn't lasted the distance, so I ordered French fries at the cafeteria. As the fries sank into the boiling oil the final boarding call for our plane crackled over the intercom. Cripes.

'Is that your plane?'

I nodded.

'One of you run out and hold the plane, the other stay here for the fries – it'll just be a couple of minutes.'

I rushed to the gate. It was already locked. I banged on the door. An airport worker in a fluorescent vest opened it. 'There's one more coming,' I panted. 'Don't lock the door.'

I raced across the runway. The flight attendant furiously waved me up the metal stairs. 'There's one more coming,' I panted. 'Don't let the plane leave.'

I stood at the top of the stairs, half out of the plane so the flight attendant couldn't lunge for the door and lock it. Ken sprinted across the runway, fries tucked under one arm, and rushed up the steps. We fell into the only available seats. The smell of freshly cooked fries filled the cabin. Other passengers gave us you-kept-us-waiting-for-fries? looks. The fries were tasty, but not tasty enough to risk a night on the tiles in Inuvik.

The Lonesome Highway, Part I

' Are we there yet? '

Us, in the Beast, somewhere in Alberta

Retracing a route already roamed is never desirable on a road trip, but we have no choice. We have to retrieve the Beast. The black Lincoln glides back down the highway from Dawson City to Whitehorse. We stop at Moose Creek Lodge to talk on a working telephone up a tree and, in the absence of any real moose, admire some moose sculpted from logs.

Rushing rivers, falls, rapids, canyons, lakes flash past. At Whitehorse we bid our hosts a fond farewell and board the bus armed with twenty-eight dollars' worth of transmission fluid, Stop Leak and a funnel. An icy rain falls from a glum sky. Two Kashmiri men heading for Calgary talk and sing and snack on a cold roast chicken carcass well into the long wet night. It smells like the last meal on earth. Payback time for the fries.

There's a brown bear, says the driver's voice from somewhere in the dark. Some bison. A moose. But rain smudges the windows and there's nothing to see but shadows and murk. Curled up on the seat I sleep until shaken awake.

Two-thirty in the morning. Fort Nelson. We drag our bags down the highway, across the road in the rain to a motel. The proprietor stands half asleep in her nightshirt. She recites the motel's amenities. 'Breakfast is free we have biscuits cereal yoghurt fruit salad toast muffins and you can order something from the hot grill bacon sausage pancakes...'

There's a rushing in my ears. I want to lie down on the motel reception floor and sleep, sleep, sleep.

In the morning the rain stops. The biscuits cereal bacon sausage breakfast waits as promised. The man behind the counter overhears us talking about picking up the Beast from Marl.

'Are you sure you have the papers for that car, sir? Never trust a white man in a white beard.'

Marl stops work on his latest project, a sideways-riding bicycle, when he sees us and takes us to the Beast. Anointed with transmission fluid and Stop Leak it's none the worse for its incarceration. It starts on the first turn of the key. Back down we go, down the world famous Alaska Highway, away from purply pink fireweed sprung up amongst the trees and spikes of Indian paintbrush, tipped red, through canola fields near Fort St John, stopping only to buy wine and blueberries and check for squirts under the car. The investment in the four litres of transmission oil, the bottle of Stop Leak and the funnel fends off further disaster. At least for now.

Once we're through British Columbia into Alberta the rain stops. The pyramids of hay wear shower caps to keep out the wet. The price of petrol drops a lot, the temperature rises a little. Drivers stick to the Beast's rear bumper like burrs on a mule's bum. Dodge Rams, the muscular, tall, wide vehicle of choice, zoom by going 40 kilometres per hour over the speed limit. As they pass, their drivers wave and give the Beast the thumbs up, which is much friendlier than waving other digits. Freight trains rattle alongside us, 65 cars, 120 cars, boxcar piled on boxcar, a moving canvas for graffiti vandals. The trains whistle loud and cheerful at the crossings. Ken trumpets the Beast's horns in return. There's more digit waving from the train drivers.

It's cold outside but the heater blows hot air all the time so inside it's warm, too warm, drowsy-making, and we've a long way to go. To keep himself awake Ken sings his own version of Roger Miller's hobo tune: 'Trailers for sale or rent, rooooms still at fifty cents'. He is king of the road again.

In Grande Prairie we drive round and round looking for a transmission shop to fix the Beast, but it's nearly noon on Saturday, everything's closed until Monday. The prospect of spending the weekend in Grande Prairie is not appealing, not when we can drive and drive some more, Beast willing, and put enough asphalt beneath the wheels to close in on the Rocky Mountains. So it's south on Highway 40, the Bighorn Highway, where the only big horns are not on sheep but on logging trucks. After stands of lissom birches with fireweed at their feet it's back to pine territory again, nothing but unlovely pines and I thought we'd left them all up north where they belong. We're on a treadmill to eternity.

'Are we there yet?' says the driver.

'Are we there yet?' says the navigator.

There are no birds, no gophers, no coyotes. A lone deer wanders out of the trees looking vaguely puzzled, as if it accidentally got into a deer transporter in a daisy meadow somewhere and ended up in Pine Hell. We argue over something really important at the time and totally forgotten since, and drive a hundred kilometres in a peeved and ruffled silence.

Lunch stop at Sheep Creek provincial recreation area, by a sheepless creek. It's eerily quiet save for a single chittering squirrel. We're the only lunchers. We eat a quick snack, keeping a watchful eye out for bears.

In the cleft of the yellow hills near Grande Cache there's a coal mine, its tubes and stacks blotting the sky and coughing up black tailings for the H. R. Milner generating station. The road slopes up, at last, into some pineless mini-mountains. The Beast leaks transmission oil but not much. Not very much at all. We creak out of the car at Grande Cache, a pretty mountain town, an old trappers' town, where adventure tourists now fish on rivers Iroquois trappers from Montréal once drifted down in canoes. Inside the tourism centre, amongst the stuffed bighorn sheep and bears with scythes for claws and solemn snowy owls and pelts of many dead things tourists are allowed to touch, including, oh woe, coyotes, there's a trayful of jade pendants.

'These are New Zealand Maori designs,' I say to the girl behind the counter. 'Where did they come from?'

'I really don't know,' she says, and backs up as if I'm about to leap over the counter and choke the information out of her.

Near Muskeg River we swerve down a bush track for a respectful pause at wooden aboriginal spirit houses built over ancient graves to give them shelter and peace. They're overlooking a river on one side but a highway on the other so peace is a scarce commodity.

We're constantly on the lookout for deer. A deer could be hiding anywhere in the steep ditches. It's a very strange thing. Whenever a deer startles out of the ditch it runs straight for a car, as if it had magnets for bones.

At Hinton there's another decision to make. Turn west on the Yellowhead Highway and drive to Edmonton, where we'll almost certainly find a new transmission and put an end to the suspense of 'Will we or won't we totally break down in some deserted, bear-infested spot?' Or drive onwards into the mountains, the glorious Rocky Mountains. I can see them, a wavering blue line on the far horizon.

Tomorrow is my birthday. I don't want to go to Edmonton, don't want to sit around some smelly transmission shop flipping through car magazines (although it's the last chance for shopping and fantasy beds at the West Edmonton Mall). I want to go into the Rockies. Ken does too. We don't ask the Beast what it wants. We just go.

Bear Scares

' Bear spray works in about 70 per cent of cases, but it might just annoy a grizzly. '

Ranger, Jasper National Park, Alberta

In 1966 my parents packed their five children in a 1963 Pontiac Safari station wagon and pointed west. All of us were younger than ten and all, except the youngest two, prone to spectacular motion sickness even in bend-free Saskatchewan. Towing a *Popular Mechanics* design, painstakingly home-built (on my father's blood and sweat) pop-up camper trailer, whose only fault was a rare but homicidal tendency to lurch toward the nearest ditch on a curve, we headed for Vancouver, 1600 kilometres and countless roadside spews in the distance.

This was our family's very first big trip out of Saskatchewan. For us kids, it was almost as exciting as getting a dog. Like most prairie chickens I'd seen hills but never a mountain, lakes but not the sea. For our parents, it must have been hell on wheels. My sisters and I each wanted a turn in the front seat, needed a pee, a drink, a cookie, then a post-drink and -cookie puke, also taken in turns. Then another pee (never needed at the same time as the puke). The heat rolling in waves off the asphalt baked eyeballs and sucked car radiators dry.

A couple of days and one whole province later we spotted a black bear cub in the ditch. I'm not suggesting that a few hundred kilometres of listening to their offspring beg for cookies dried up my parents' urge to protect the flock, but as we bear-snacks-on-legs tumbled out of the car and headed for the cub they waved and locked the doors. Not true of course. One of my parents took a photo of us three skinny-legged girls gazing at the bear (my veterinarian-to-be sister Colette grinning like a goose, me in elbows-up flight mode, my doctor-to-be sister Dianne pondering the risks), and the bear cub – not much more than a couple of arms' lengths away – gazing at us. I can only presume our other parent waited nearby with our two younger juicier siblings, armed with a penknife or a large rock in case Mama Bear charged up. She didn't. We got back in the car, body parts intact, and drove on – until one of us needed a drink and a cookie, a pee and a puke.

Rolling relentlessly down the last few kilometres towards Jasper National Park and bear territory, Ken and I tortured each other with the 'Bear attacks human' stories my relatives had so enthusiastically shared, along the lines of hapless campers scalped, dragged and – still shrieking – gnawed on for days while their partner cowered in a tree, shrivelling from starvation. Ken isn't afraid of much – heights, snakes, lingerie departments – except being eaten alive by bears, sharks, cougars or anything else with teeth like saws and fleshy breath. I had a fear of watching someone being eaten alive.

In unfanged, clawless New Zealand we'd grown used to cavorting carefree along bushy nature trails where there was nothing more worrisome than the kauri snail, 'a slow nocturnal carnivore...the fear and dread of the forest worms', as one Department of Conservation sign poetically put it. As long as New Zealand trampers trotted along faster than forest worms, there was little to fear or dread.

Canadian backwoods, though, needed a full anti-carnivore arsenal. By the time we reached the Jasper Park visitor centre, bears with ill intent lurked behind every fir tree. The visitor centre heaved with Germans, Japanese and Americans waving maps and wanting to know the best, easiest, closest place to see bears, moose, mountain goats and other forest critters. I waited my turn, idly flicking through a pamphlet demanding, 'Have you seen this toad?'

I had bigger concerns than renegade amphibians.

'Now, about this bear business,' I said to the ranger behind the counter.

'If you take the normal precautions, the chances of an encounter are small.'

He handed me a Parks Canada bear-safety pamphlet. A bald-headed ranger reared up behind him, made grizzly bear faces, growled and sunk back down again.

'Store your food away from your tent,' advised the first ranger, ignoring his deranged colleague. 'Carry bear bells and make noise when hiking. Only one trail is closed right now because of bear problems.'

Bear problems, ha. My guess was they were still cleaning up the remains of a couple of scalpless, disembowelled hikers. But I thanked him and found a seat to peruse the pamphlet.

It left a lot of questions unanswered. 'It is unlawful to feed or approach wildlife.' This assumed there would be enough of you left after feeding or approaching a bear to slap handcuffs on. 'All bears are dangerous. Stay in your vehicle if encountered.' Yes, but you can't live in your car forever, even if it's a heavy metal bear-proof Chevy. 'Bear spray can be effective with some bears when used properly.' Which bears? Do they know who they are? Just how close did you have to be for bear spray to work?

I trotted back to the counter.

'What about bear spray?'

'It's pepper spray. You can buy it at any sports shop in town.'

'Fine, but does it work?'

The ranger shuffled a paper on the counter. 'In about seventy per cent of cases, it works. But you have to be within five metres of the bear. It might just annoy a grizzly.'

This reminded me of a bear joke posted on the wall at the Fort Nelson museum. 'Acquaint yourself with the differences between a black bear and a grizzly bear. Familiarise yourself with the scat. A black bear's droppings are full of squirrel fur and berries. A grizzly bear's droppings are full of jingly bells and smell like pepper.'

This was ha ha, funny, but not comforting. A piffling canister of pepper spray didn't seem like much of an armament, especially if the hiker had to get within a sniff of a grizzly's armpits to fire it. And then it might get right up his nose. Where were the puncture-proof body armour, the erectable chain-link fence for each campsite and the long weapon with something lethal at the end of it? In Old Crow the canoeing couple we'd met carried not only pepper spray but a twelve-gauge shotgun loaded with blanks and, if all else failed, real, bearhide-penetrating shells.

We found a sporting goods shop on Jasper's main street and,

body armour being in short supply, bought a can of bear repellent labelled as dog repellent. I snapped a bear bell on to the daypack. Jingling like Santa's little reindeer I felt ready to go out into the woods, preferably at the forefront of slower, fatter, tastier walkers.

Jasper is the largest of the six mountain parks, one of the oldest – almost a century – and, for my money, the best. Best waterfalls, best mountains, best ice fields, best wildlife-spotting. Within a few kilometres of leaving Jasper village we'd clocked up roadside encounters with a clutch of daft-looking bighorn sheep, a herd of caribou grazing the greenery and one smirking coyote trotting along just out of photographic range.

The park brochure rated the Maligne Canyon trail as a mostly level, easy outing, despite its onerous name, courtesy of a nineteenth-century French Canadian Jesuit priest who lost his worldly bits and bobs crossing the wicked river he called *maligne*. And so it seemed: a pleasant dawdle along the Maligne and Athabasca Rivers over limestone boulders and under long-limbed pines. Ken dropped a stick over the side of a bridge into water rushing along like a frothy green drain fifteen metres below. The stick turned to toothpicks in seconds.

An elderly Japanese tourist contemplated the stick's splintered remains. 'If my glasses fall in will you jump down and get them for me?' he asked Ken. 'You're young and strong.'

Oh how we laughed and only briefly thought about pushing the cheeky old devil overboard.

On the way back the trail climbed deceptively but steadily uphill. It was fine for the first five minutes. Then it wasn't fine at all. I wheezed. I gasped. I dripped sweat and trembled. My legs mutinied; my knees bent east and west. I sank slowly earthward. A mum pushing a pram passed me on the trail, followed briskly by a hundred-year-old Chinese lady and a flabby fellow in city shoes carrying a Pomeranian dog in a Pomeranian-coloured bag. Someone, I discovered, had swapped my lungs and knees for inferior models while I sat eating bonbons in the Beast.

'What's the matter?' Ken had been springing up the rocks like a mountain goat. He sprang back down to where I sat on a rock, quietly becoming one with the moss.

'Altitude,' I lied.

A baby in nappies crawled past. It was a nasty shock. If a bear did loom out of the woods, the last bit of bear-bait left panting in the dust, behind the toddlers, old folks and dog walkers, would be me.

Beauty Creek was precisely that: a pristine sparkling ribbon racing towards the foot of a snowy peak.

'Trangia time,' said Ken, who liked a milky coffee to sharpen his driving and bear-spotting skills in the afternoon. The little camp stove had performed so faithfully on the European trip it'd come along for this ride too. The coffee bubbled in the pot, the creek tinkled over stones. All that loveliness, without having to walk more than a step or two. Unlike the Columbia Icefield, the next scenic viewpoint, which again required putting one foot in front of the other up a hill. I trudged up the smooth broad shoulder of frozen glacial water, punch drunk on the cracking blue sky, wind flash-freezing the cheeks, eyes stinging from the glare of light flaring off the largest patch of ice south of the Arctic Circle. It was blue, and bare, and beautiful. I trudged down and sat gasping in the car for many minutes wondering where the nearest oxygen bar might be.

While I reinflated my lungs Ken added the Beast to a clutch of cars stopped along the highway. Hoping for a moose I crawled out.

'What's everyone looking at?'

A stout matron peering through binoculars pointed. 'A bear.'

A black hairy hind leg waved up and down behind a fir tree. A bear doing callisthenics. Oh, good. As if a flabby bear wasn't enough to worry about, here was one toning up for sprints. I sighed, knowing I likely couldn't outrun even the stout matron if the bear made a lunge for us. I crawled back in the car to rustle up the map and find a camping spot before night fell.

Rampart Creek, just over the border in Banff National Park,

was rated 'primitive' – no showers, no running water, no park ranger to hide behind when the going got gruesome. In the low dusk we backed the Chevy under a canopy of firs close to the composting toilets (the shorter the distance as scampering prey, the better) but far from the bear-proof rubbish bins.

Ken went off in search of the water pump. I picked up the bear-safety pamphlet while stirring dinner. It gave additional helpful advice: 'Speak to the bear calmly ('Nice fur coat! Have a nice day!'), play dead (if you surprise a bear), or try to escape (if the bear attacks you).' Harsh penalties for getting it wrong. Ears nearly twirling off our heads as we listened for bear-decibel snorts or snuffles, we sat down at a picnic table imprinted with a drawing of a bear. There was just no getting away from them.

While we ate, a backpacking camper, Steve from British Columbia, set up a distinctly not bear-proof tent next to us. In the bear versus human debate Steve sided passionately with the hairy ones.

'It's not the bears' fault,' argued Steve, waving a tent peg for emphasis. 'Bears were here first. More and more people are taking over their territory, and they have nowhere to go. People do really stupid things, too, like keep food in their tents or get too close trying to pet the cubs.'

I agreed that was a really stupid thing.

Steve continued: 'A ranger told me more than a hundred grizzly bears have been killed over the last thirty years around here because they were labelled 'problem bears', or got hit by cars or trains. It's not fair for bears.'

Steve had a point. When the bears finally stood up en masse and roared 'Vive la révolution!' I hoped he'd be spared.

The knowledge that bears had just cause for grievance made me even more jittery and paranoid. After a quick toilet run and tooth brushing I wormed into the back of the Chevy and locked the doors. Long after Ken's soft snores huffled the air I lay, eyes wide open, waiting for the screech of vengeful bear claws peeling back the car roof as easily as lifting the lid on a tin of quivering sardines.

A paltry few hours later I awoke from a clammy nervous sleep.

Smuts, Saskatchewan The Beast basks beneath the onion-shaped domes of Holy Trinity Ukrainian Orthodox church, one of two in a town with mysteriously absent townsfolk.

opposite **Vegreville, Alberta** Ken admires the world's largest Ukrainian Easter egg – the ultimate in egg art – and imagines the giant chook that laid it.

above **Pelly Crossing, Yukon Territory** Festooned with moose antlers outside, papered with travellers' tales inside, these loos are a welcome bush retreat.

below **Dawson City, Yukon Territory** Wooden boardwalks over dirt streets run in front of shops selling everything from grizzly-bear keychains to lattes.

left / below left Here a wooden moose, there a moose sign – show us the moose!

below / below right Traveller's hazards: sled dog's revenge in **Old Crow, Yukon Territory**; gophers everywhere.

opposite **Wanuskewin, Saskatchewan** Beaded and boned, feathered and fringed Roberta, a Cree First Nations dancer, takes a break.

opposite below **Jasper National Park, Alberta** The glorious Rocky Mountains.

above Drumheller, Alberta Toothy *T. rex* shakes, rattles and roars.
below Wayne, Alberta Last Chance to slake a summer thirst in a wild west saloon.
opposite above Saskatoon, Saskatchewan Jellybean Chevys all in a row.
opposite below Madge Lake, Saskatchewan Taking a tailgate break in the comfy Beast.

above left Winnipeg, Manitoba Cosying up to one of the Bears on Broadway is the closest I want to get to a polar bear.

above right White River, Ontario The coldest spot in Canada – or is it?

below Niagara Falls, Ontario A Maid of the Mist boat takes wet falls watchers under the rainbow towards the thundering colossus.

In the blackness I could hear nothing, see nothing. Nothing at all. Just a creepy nothingness. If a twig crackled or a branch snapped, that'd be something. I'd know the bear's whereabouts. This silence had a sinister watchfulness in it. I pulled the pillow over my head, waited, waited, tired myself out from waiting, and slept.

At dawn's light on this summer's morn the thermometer read 3°C inside the car. I bundled up in sheepskin coat, possum gloves and socks, a wool hat and a thick scarf to keep the chill from seeping into my very eyeballs. Ken poked his head out of the sleeping bag.

'I dreamt a bear was breaking into the car.' He shuddered. 'I threw a hand grenade at it.'

Damn. Why hadn't we brought any grenades?

Clinging dew dampened the picnic table, the car and the ground. We shivered out of bed into air only a couple of degrees colder than inside the car.

'Look at that,' said Ken.

'What?'

'That.'

He pointed to a dry patch just behind the Beast's rear bumper shaped in a lazy 'U' with a fat bit at the back. Even folk with the imagination of a tree stump could see what it clearly was – the outline of a bear's round bottom, legs poked out in front.

There are times when it's best to sit a while, make a thoughtful cup of cocoa and ponder life's little mysteries. Such as, if a bear had sat behind us in the night why didn't he just smash the window and snack on our innards? What was he doing, flipping through recipes? Or eyeing up Steve's tent as a better bet? This was not one of those times. We leapt back in the car – which started, as always, magnificently – and sped away from dark spooky woods and vampire-ish morning chill sucking the life out of innocent campers, and things that sit on their fat furry rumps in the night.

The planned drive to Vancouver on the west coast was not to be. Despite generous oil transfusions, the Chevy's transmission slowly but purposefully leaked its life's blood onto the nation's highways. It didn't seem fair to force the Beast to limp further west. We reluctantly decided to skip Vancouver and head back to the familiarity of Saskatoon for a transmission transplant, tired old heap permitting.

One obstacle stood in the way: Kicking Horse Pass, Canada's most famous mountain pass. A big hill had unhinged the Chevy's transmission in the first place, and another bunch of big hills was not about to get out of the road just for us.

Legend had it that in 1858 Scotsman James Hector, a geologist attached to a Canadian Pacific Railway (CPR) expedition, went searching on horseback for a passage through the fortress-like Rockies. One of the grumpy mounts kicked him in the ribs, breaking three and knocking him unconscious. The geologist's aboriginal guides gave him up for dead and carted him off to a suitable burial place. The geologist, rudely bounced back into the land of the living, had a Eureka moment when he awoke to see a slit in the rocks through which CPR could sling its railroad and connect east to west. James Hector, perhaps also tired of winter, later emigrated to New Zealand to take on the Southern Alps and become the eponym for the rare, winsome Hector's dolphin. This might have made up for missing out to a horse in the 'name the mountain pass' game.

Not too much later British adventurer John Foster Fraser rode down the pass on the cow-catcher of a CPR steam locomotive. He breathlessly described the ride in his 1905 book *Canada As It Is*: 'Reeling, screeching at the curves, with mocking echoes thrown back, whirling into a danksome tunnel, and yelling all the way, plunging like a runaway – why, the man on the cow-catcher has to grip tight, hold his lips tight, as with swoop the descent is made.'

After fleeing Rampart Creek we'd ventured downhill through the pass for a look at some falls in Yoho National Park and, in the town of Golden, more relly-visiting. Downhill didn't stress the Beast's transmission. Uphill might. Ken girded the Beast's loins with more oil. The Beast chugged up the pass at a sedate but steady rate. At the top Ken checked for signs of meltdown. The transmission puddle remained a puddle, not a lake. So far, so good. Then came the descent, which we seemed to be making with some swoop of our own. Under the Beast's wheels the road whizzed along uncomfortably close to the cliff edge.

'You're going kind of fast. What's that smell?' I said.

'What smell?'

'I smell something. Like hot metal.'

'Well…could be the brakes.'

'What! I thought Bruce fixed those.'

'He did. But they're old-style drum brakes, not disc brakes. It's not good to ride drum brakes down a steep hill. They can fade. Bruce thought we should replace the drums with disc brakes, remember?'

I did. Still suffering from shock to the wallet we'd stuck with the antique-style brakes that now held us cheapskates to the road. Still, there was no other way down, short of jumping out of the car and landing on the cow-catcher of a CPR locomotive.

'So why didn't I smell that smell on the other side?'

'We had to stop for all that road construction. No chance to build up speed.'

I gripped tight, held my lips tight. A couple of brake-testing whooshes around corners, down a thundering straight – home free.

Hutterite Homes and Ancient Bones

' We're just the same as people
on the Outside. '

Elizabeth, Fairview Hutterite Colony, Alberta

Growing up in Saskatoon I'd often see truckloads of Hutterites coming to town for Thursday-night shopping. The stolid solid men with hands that could juggle watermelons, dressed in black suits hooked and suspendered but not buttoned; the women plain in handmade headscarves and dark dresses with modestly patterned aprons over top, whispering together in German. In the sixties Hutterite men sometimes appeared at the kitchen door selling freshly dead chickens. Hutterites farmed communally on swathes of prime land throughout southern Alberta and Saskatchewan. For that reason, as well as their outmoded dress sense, these folk seemed alien, unreachable and just plain strange.

The German Hutterite religious movement was started more than four centuries ago by Jakob Hutter, who met a nasty end roasted at the stake in Innsbruck as a heretic. The pacifist Hutterites dodged religious persecution during the Reformation throughout Eastern Europe, finally washing up on US shores in the 1800s. They fled to Canada during World War I with anti-German sentiment snapping at their heels. Since then the Hutterites had quietly got on with acquiring more and more land until their colonies achieved near town-like status.

The question was, how did we get inside one of the closed communities for a visit?

You can just drive in, said veterinary friends in Crossfield, Alberta, who ministered to a nearby Hutterite colony's animal needs. Tell them we said hello.

The Beast had barely nudged into the car park at the Fairview colony when a smiling bespectacled young woman emerged from a low concrete building. I asked about a tour.

'Of course. We get lots of buses coming here, mostly from the US, lots of school kids.'

After a lifetime of thinking of Hutterites as Mysterious Religious Cult, Hutterites as Top Tourist Attraction came as a bit of a shock.

She asked where we were from. 'Saskatoon,' I said, to avoid lengthy explanations about how we could possibly be from somewhere like New Zealand while sounding exactly like Saskatonians.

This stirred up some excitement. 'Have you been to the Hillcrest colony there? Our sister moved there after she got married. We haven't seen her since.'

Hutterites, she explained, were baptised at age eighteen and could marry after that. Marriage was usually to a mate from another colony, and women moved to their husband's colony. All married men grew beards, although no specimens on display at Fairview approached a Marl Brown plushiness.

The young woman showed us the industrial-strength laundry and commercial-sized ovens where women toiled away baking sixty loaves twice a week for the colony's men, women and children. It smelled as divine as only fresh bread can.

'That's a lot of bread. Is there any for sale?'

Alas, no. There were forty mouths to feed.

All the colony's children ate together until they were fifteen. Adults ate in another room, with males and females at separate tables. Colonies were split in two like amoeba once they reached fifty or so people.

'Do you mind taking the rest of the tour with my mother? I must keep up with the laundry.'

Rosy-cheeked Elizabeth appeared and continued as if she'd been conducting the tour all along. She led us through her own immaculate home, one of several set around a square of precision-cut lawn. Caught by surprise in a room full of handmade Hutterite souvenirs for sale, I resisted the cushions, rugs and socks but caved in on the duck-patterned tea towel. Across the compound we poked through hangar-sized barns full to the rafters with state-of-the-art tractors and combines shiny enough to shave in. Ken's jaw bounced a few times on the spick-and-span floor. Like many good prairie lads he's a tractor connoisseur. These were some of the finest Massey Fergusons ever to roll across a wheat field.

Elizabeth listed the colony's other wealth. It was enough to bring tears to the eyes of would-be farmers contemplating life on a plot with the odd chook or piglet. 'We own six thousand acres planted in barley, oats, wheat and canola. There are three thousand hogs, fifteen thousand chickens, also dairy cows. We butcher three thousand chickens every eight weeks and sell them at markets.'

At the abattoir the chicken-rendering area was, like everything else, Germanically spotless. Not a sniff of poultry death lingered anywhere. Next door to the abattoir a woman and two little girls in head scarves stemmed cherries for canning. Spotting the camera they struck a photogenic pose. Times had definitely changed.

'All of the children, there are six in the colony at the moment, are home schooled. We speak German until age six then learn English, but we speak German amongst ourselves. Young people do leave but most come back.'

It wasn't surprising that some young people left. No television, radio or movies were allowed. Socialising was mostly done with other colonies. Colonists attend church every day.

I wondered if people from the Outside ever made their way Inside.

'Not many, but if someone wants to learn our ways and work, there are plenty of jobs.'

Men built everything from canning bins to incinerators to metal clothes horses to the houses and every bit of furniture in them. The women sanded and finished the beds, dressers, tables and hope chests for the time when they too set off for colonies afar armed with duck-patterned tea towels.

But in such a close community, surely there was the odd biff or tiff? Elizabeth was predictably diplomatic. If there was any brawling going on, Outsiders weren't to know about it. 'We do have disagreements but you have to comb out the weeds, just like a garden. We're just the same as people on the Outside.'

Maybe not just the same, but in Hutterite colonies like Fairview the gap between Inside and Outside had shrunk. Still, when the apocalypse thundered down upon all of us citified folk who didn't know one end of a chicken from the other, Hutterites would tidy up the mess, build a new barn and carry on plucking.

Alberta, I'd come to believe, had some of the Best in the West attractions – best petrol prices (important for V8s), best national park (Jasper) and so far best Giant Roadside Thing (the Vegreville egg), for which they are forgiven all those northern pines and the demise of Kelly's Bar. The Alberta weather had also ripened to a fine summer swelter.

Not content with this bounty, Alberta was also the dinosaur capital of the world. At Drumheller there was a giant *T. rex* or two to prove it. But first, before the tyrannosauruses, I wanted a look at a 70-million-year-old fossil bed. A skip down the highway from the Fairview Hutterite Colony landed us at the rim of Horseshoe Canyon, which may well have been shaped like the shoe of a horse but this was difficult to tell from the ground. This was doubtless the reason for the helicopter tours buzzing the sky every few minutes. The choppers didn't detract from the canyon's striated gorgeousness. I stood on the edge and wholeheartedly admired the stupendous geological trifle of sandstone, mudstone and coal. But not for long. Big Dino beckoned.

'Do you know where to find this thing?' Ken was keener to hunt down a latte and a spade-sized slice of pie than a fake dinosaur.

'It's the word's largest dinosaur. How hard can it be?'

Not hard at all. The mighty *T. rex* snarling above the tourist information centre was of exceptional toothy ugliness, as a *T. rex* should be. I paid a loonie or two to clamber up inside the monster's staircase gullet. In the darkest scariest parts of the climb the creature roared and shook and scared little kids, and some big ones, into howling messes. After I patted my hair back down and gave thanks Ken was not around to hear me scream like a seven-year-old, I stepped into the behemoth's gaping maw for the best view in the land, about twelve puny human lengths above its three-toed feet and far across the badlands sheltering the bones of its real relatives.

'How was it?' said Ken, blissfully replete with pie.

'Good. Nice view.'

'I'll bet you screamed like a seven-year-old,' said Ken.

Drumheller's devotion to dinosaurs spawned places like the Jurassic Inn and a colourful spattering of dinosaur statues on street corners, in parks and campgrounds. Here a gorgosaurus, there a stegosaurus, everywhere a triceratops. These, of course, were just cutesy models to get visitors in the mood for the real thing, which held court at the Royal Tyrrell Museum of Palaeontology, a short and sweaty drive from Drumheller's town centre. The genuine older-than-everybody-on-earth skeletons of tyrannosaurus rex, albertosaurus and gigantosaurus, plus the bones of woolly mammoths and many other ancient critters, clearly proved a couple of points. First, bears are mere carnivore midgets sized up against these once-were megamonsters. Also, we all look better with our skin on.

What the hundreds, if not thousands, of other 'saurus-struck patrons packed in cheek-by-jowl thought I couldn't say. But if the old carnivores suddenly sprung to life there'd be no shortage of shrieking snacks for lunch.

'How old are they? Where do they live? What do they eat?' a rambunctious tot trying to climb onto the old bones yelled at his mother.

'Bad boys who don't do what they're told,' snapped the harried parent.

On the other side of Drumheller, on the road to East Coulee, a crop of sandstone hoodoos drew crowds of a quieter sort. The vanilla-and-chocolate pillars in quirksome shapes wore harder capstones, like mushroom hats, that kept the sandstone underneath from dissolving in the rain. It was the sort of place trolls might gambol about under a full moon. Under the full noonday sun gambolling was out. An ice-cold drink at a saloon was in, although eleven single-lane bridges stood between us and a beer at the Last Chance Saloon in the town of Wayne. These bridges gained for the tiny town Guinness World Records fame for most single-lane bridges in the shortest distance. It did make me think the Guinness people had a lot to answer for, encouraging such promiscuous bridge-building and centuries of matrimony.

Wayne, like the Yukon mining towns, was a mere shadow of its former coal-mining self. The Last Chance Saloon, though, stuck hard and fast to the flavour of a rootin' tootin' old-time bar, albeit without the saddle stools we seemed doomed never to sit upon. The owner had obviously caught the same packrat fever as his counterpart Mike Mancini up in Keno City. Barely a scrap of wall could be seen through the old bits of mining equipment and deer heads. We sipped a cold beer under racks of antlers while contemplating the bullet hole in the ceiling reminding customers to pay up, or else.

On the highway east from Drumheller the plains rose up and swallowed the valley of the dinosaurs. I glanced back through the tailgate window. There was nothing to see but canola fields. In a trick of terrain the badlands, like the dinosaurs, had vanished.

The Chevy's transmission still squirted and dribbled. But Kicking Horse Pass hadn't killed it, so chances were good it would hold together for the last flat stretch to home base.

'Do you think we'll make it?'

'No worries, mate,' said Ken.

On we forged, past Chinook and Cereal and Oyen, stopping only to squeeze in the last tank of cheap Alberta petrol. The Guess Who's seventies anthem 'Running Back to Saskatoon', about gas stations, grease monkeys and workin' on cars, thumped through my head like *T. rex* footsteps for every one of those five hundred kilometres.

Showtime in Toon Town

' The drive-in was the place to go in summer with your honey. '

Karen, author and drive-in enthusiast, Saskatoon, Saskatchewan

The Beast needed not just minor surgery but a full transmission transplant if we were to drive the rest of the trip without buying shares in Stop Leak manufacturers and worrying about every hill higher than a gopher mound. Since we'd arrived in town on a long weekend the operation couldn't be performed for days. So we did what all car owners with bench seats should do at least once in their lives – go with your sweetie to a drive-in movie.

Drive-ins literally loomed large in my Saskatoon upbringing. In the early years our family lived on Saskatoon's outskirts behind the Star Trailer Court, in a 'work in progress' home my hardworking father crafted together when he wasn't putting out the town's fires.

This was a place of childhood wonders. To the north, the trailer court heaved with other kids to play with like my pal Beverly Sidebottom, one of a tomboy pack duty-bound to teach other kids how to eat worms and dirt. To the south, the soft-drink bottling plant across the dirt street handed out cola and orange drink to thirsty kids as long as we returned the bottles. I drank so much cola I threw up in the Saskatoon berry bushes and never drank it again. To the west the Skyway Drive-In Theatre rose from a grassy field like a square-rigged prairie sail.

On summer evenings my sisters and I sat warming our pyjama-clad bottoms on the concrete patio behind the house. From across the field Bugs Bunny tangoed with Elmer Fudd on a screen as wide as the sky. Who needed sound? Anyone could learn to lip read a three-metre rabbit. A decade later the drive-in was the place to go in summer with your honey to drink beer, pash like rabbits and, if things got boring, watch the movies. There was a sense of ritual to it all. Pick a spot outside spying distance of anybody else. Pull the car up on the slope so you can see out of the windscreen. Roll down the window a crack, take the speaker off the pole, hang it on the window. Send the boyfriend to buy popcorn. Watch the movie. Or pash like rabbits. In late summer the aurora borealis, the shimmery northern lights, ghost danced pink and green in the heavens. Moviegoers got out of their cars to stand like gophers watching the best show in town.

The Skyway fell long ago to the developer's bulldozer. But to the east, the Sundown Drive-In remained, a resolute relic. Ken found a spot not too close to anybody else, mostly because hardly anybody else was there. He drove the Beast up on a grassy slope. The tinny window speakers had become, blessedly and sadly, a thing of the past. I tuned the radio to the appropriate station (giving thanks the Beast possessed such a modern item as a radio). I sent the husband to buy popcorn.

The clientele had changed. Families of kiddies in their ducky jammies replaced drinking snogging teenagers. The woman in the next car snuggling a white poodle gave us 'what are you looking at' looks. We snuggled each other, though limbs failed to bend as limberly as I remembered in the cramp of a Chevy bench seat. We even watched some of the movie.

Over the weekend the Super Run classic car show came to town.

'You promised me two car shows,' Ken reminded me. 'To make up for the dancing.'

Fair enough, though the chromeless Beast wasn't quite pretty enough to enter a show this classy. Still, I sniffed an opportunity to flog the car to Chevy lovers at the show. What to do with the car after the trip, assuming there'd still be a car or at least parts of it left at the other end of the country, posed a problem. Shipping it back to New Zealand wasn't an option – too expensive, too big a car for the roads, too thirsty an engine for the petrol pumps, and where would we park the thing? Five motorcycles and a sidecar already fought for shed space in Auckland. That left selling the car during the trip.

I whipped up a for sale sign and stuck it in the Beast's window. Bruce had tracked down an original 1956 Chevy magazine ad online: 'Seats a whole baseball team beautifully! It's one of 6 sprightly new Chevrolet station wagons!' I stuck that on too, even though the line about the baseball team wasn't strictly true of our model, and bought a cellphone to field the calls certain to come from eager Chevy fans.

The Chevys, Mustangs, Studebakers, all five hundred of them shapely chromed wonders, made modern cars look like guinea pigs on wheels. Ken lingered over a row of Tri-Chevys in jellybean colours, muttering something that sounded suspiciously like, 'Maybe we should keep ours after all.'

The Chevys were undeniably cute but I fell hard and fast in love with a Cadillac. Not just any Cadillac, mind you. A 1959 Cadillac Biarritz. Seminole Red with fins as broad as the tail of a whale, twin bullet tail lights and enough chrome on the jewelled grille to build a city. Only about 1300 of these plane-sized lovelies had ever rolled off the production line.

'Would you like to sit in it?' asked a hovering fellow a decade or so older than the car. 'Took me nine years to restore. It's nineteen feet long and eighty-one inches wide. I need a security guard to watch it every time I take it out.'

It was an honour and a privilege, a true moose moment, to sit on pure heavenly white eighty-one-inch-wide leather upholstery.

But expensive cars didn't impress Ken. 'They'll still get a flat tyre. The owner will still pick his nose.'

I didn't care. Next time the Beast kicked up a fuss, I was leaving it for a Caddie.

The chrome clips had arrived as promised. Armed with a cordless drill and an even temper Ken once again retreated to the garage and set about sticking the clips and the many miles of chrome back on. I took on the job of keeping up with important current affairs missed while travelling. The *Saskatoon StarPhoenix* newspaper routinely reported interesting news items.

An ice hockey player skated through an entire game with a stowaway mouse in the toe of his skate. The mouse survived the game but not the locker room round up.

Police in Moose Jaw arrested a male burglar wearing a stolen bikini and carrying a mannequin. Police said the man 'was in bad need of a good waxing'. The motive was unknown 'and the mannequin's not saying anything'.

Canada's public health system was in crisis. Was the federal health minister the right man to protect medicare? 'Is Colonel Sanders a friend of chickens?' asked an opposition MP.

An ice-fishing Polish priest hooked a record 8–kilogram walleye in northern Saskatchewan while jigging and reciting the Canticle of Mary. Months later his father hooked a 6–kilogram walleye on the same lake while praying his fourth Hail Mary.

Skunks pounced on a subscriber's newspaper and anointed it daily with skunk juice. The subscriber decided the smelly ones were 'expressing their view of the news…They have a quick look… and decide, "Let us spray".'

And sadly a CPR freight train struck and killed the butt-nipping bear of Alberta, Bear 66, in Banff National Park. She left behind three orphaned cubs.

One day footsteps clattered on the verandah.

'Is that the Roto-Rooter man?' called my mother, who'd been wrestling with drain-plugging tree roots for some time.

The footsteps stopped. A raggedy man with a wild head of steel wool peered around the corner.

'I thought you were the sewer man,' said Mom.

'You could stick me down the drainpipe and give me a couple of twirls,' said the raggedy man.

Bernie Howgate had fetched up almost everywhere except down a drainpipe. He'd cycled across Canada in a Pakistani rickshaw. He'd kayaked the coastline of Newfoundland. Now he travelled the country door to door selling books on his adventures. Home, when he needed one, was Mud Lake in the chunk of Québec carved off to make up the Labrador part of Canada's most easterly province, Newfoundland and Labrador.

'One winter the pack ice ripped through the trees and tore a corner off my house,' said Bernie. 'We sat in the house drinking beer and watched it come. Best thing that ever happened. Somebody who knew what they were doing rebuilt the house. Now we can play darts in a straight line.'

I bought a book. Nothing, but nothing, especially a crotchety classic car, was going to keep me from Canada's farthest-flung eastern shores.

The Chevy's transmission transplant went without a hitch. On the night before departing Saskatoon the Chevy cellphone rang. Someone on the other end had spotted the for sale sign at the car show. The prospective buyer liked the Beast. He offered to do a deal on the spot. Half now, half when we'd finished the trip, providing it hadn't been bashed or smashed between now and then.

It was tempting. Very, very tempting. But fixing up the car's bad bits had sucked up an unholy pile of Canadian loonies. Plus, the sign had obviously worked a treat.

'What do you think? More would be better?'

'Maybe we should. It's a pretty good price. But more would be better,' said Ken, weary from a week of chrome clipping.

Saskatoon Chevy Fan wasn't budging.

These were early days. Seven more provinces of Chevy lovers lay ahead. We turned him down, politely and with thanks. But I kept his phone number just in case.

Camping Highs, Camping Lows

' Blame the raccoon moon. '

Camper, Madge Lake,
Saskatchewan-Manitoba border

The Beast's major transmission surgery, on top of its earlier woes, had liposuctioned any fat built into the travel schedule and the budget. We needed to clock up some big miles to put Newfoundland in our sights before the snow flew. Treating the new transmission with respect, Ken set a steady sixty miles per hour course straight towards Manitoba.

Post-transplant, the Beast seemed a much happier animal. It loved this ride. Built for bouncing over gravelly ruts on fifties roads it joyfully cleared bumps spelling death or dismemberment for newer low-slung cars. On this straight stretch Ken steered with a finger or two on the wheel, the other arm slung manfully out the window. The bench seat easily accommodated the driver sprawled behind the wheel, a fat stack of maps, a more truthful guidebook, water bottles, bags of chips and cookies, two cameras, a notebook and a box of tissues between us, and the navigator sitting cross-legged or upside-down or sideways on the passenger side trying to read the maps. For some reason, perhaps it was the panoramic windows, motion sickness wasn't a problem. I could read maps in the Beast without wanting to share my lunch with the roadside grasses.

I mark off passing towns.

Clarkboro. Cross the South Saskatchewan River on a neat little four-car cable-guided ferry. The trip only takes five minutes. The ferryman is remarkably cheerful despite spending his days taking cars on five-minute trips across the river, when there is a car.

Muenster. Locals stare at us, wordless. This is unnerving. The Chevy is universally admired – maybe this is Ford country? Lunch at the Muenster family restaurant. The waitress is remarkably cheerful despite spending her days serving near-wordless customers.

'How is everything?' she asks a customer.

'Terrible!' he says, and spoons up the last of his soup.

Quill Lake. The Goose Capital of Saskatchewan. See no geese.

Canora. Stop, peer in the window of the Toy and Autograph Museum. It is closed.

Veregin. Stop, peer around the National Doukhobor Heritage Village. It is not closed and is fully worth the stop. The Russian Doukhobors, once a communally living religious group like the Hutterites, crossed the Atlantic as the nineteenth century turned twentieth to sink their ploughs into fertile prairie soil. Frozen two metres deep and rock solid in winter, the soil wasn't having anything to do with ploughs or other man-made foolery. Before winter set in the Doukhobors scratched out caves in the banks of the North Saskatchewan River. Forty of them bravely burrowed in like badgers until in spring the ground thawed enough to hew out a more luxurious sod hut. Conscientious objectors like the Hutterites, the Doukhobors baulked at conscription for World War I, mainly protesting by peaceful means. The breakaway Sons of Freedom zealots, though, protested against all perceived ills by tearing off their clothes, marching buck naked through the streets and burning down whatever got in the way. Arson aside, this seemed a foolhardy tactic in a climate where January temperatures crack the thermometer at -40°C or lower.

Somewhere near Kamsack. There's a bright red grain elevator. Not many of these still stand on the prairies. A grain truck drives right inside. Stop, peer inside to see what happens in a grain elevator. The grain elevator operator is remarkably cheerful despite spending his days answering silly questions from tourists. This elevator is as high as several trucks laid end to end. But it's a relatively small one, holding only 4400 tonnes of grain. At nearby Yorkton the elevator holds 25,000 tonnes.

'How's farming these days?' I ask a farmer who is watching the wheat spilling out of his truck into the sorting bins that ferry the grain up the elevator to bigger storage bins.

'Not good,' harrumphs the farmer. 'Price of wheat fell from five dollars last year to two dollars per bushel this year. And the price of everything just goes up. It's not right.'

Who's to blame? Those no-account Ottawa thieves again.

On the road. Ken announces it's my turn at the wheel of the Beast. Piloting a huge car, huger than a Toyota Corolla anyway, with manual steering on the wrong side of an unfamiliar highway is not my idea of fun. I'm a distracted driver at the best of times. I'd rather daydream and rummage through the snacks. Ken wants a turn at daydreaming and rummaging through the snacks.

'I don't like it. I don't want to do it.' Whine.

'This is a straight road. There's no traffic. It's an automatic transmission. What can go wrong? Just steer and stick to the right. This right, not the other right.'

Fair is fair. I slide behind the chrome-and-bakelite wheel. It's the size of a tractor tyre but the Beast is surprisingly easy to steer. I almost enjoy it. This tempts fate too far. Ken suggests we stop for petrol. I signal to turn left. No, I don't. I hit the column gear shifter instead of the turn signal. The expensive new transmission snaps smartly from drive into reverse at thirty miles per hour. The Beast convulses and dies like a gutted gopher in the middle of the highway. The only car for five hundred kilometres screeches to a stop centimetres from the rear bumper.

'Feck!' says Ken. 'What are you doing!'

'I'm driving!'

On sweaty attempt number three, or maybe three hundred, I restart the car and turn left ('this left, not the other left') into the petrol station. A few strong words are spoken. I flounce out of the driver's seat and regain my rightful place as passenger. To the relief of all concerned I do not drive the car one more metre during the entire trip.

The Beast suffered no internal injuries from this mishap. It carried on without protest to the evening's camping destination at Madge Lake in Duck Mountain Provincial Park, on the Manitoba border.

The most easterly camping trip my family ever took was to this very park. Once again we towed the camper trailer, which behaved much better when asked only to head in a perfectly straight track. Our springer spaniel Molly rode in the car. Two pet guinea pigs, Jaycie and Percy, came along in a large outdoor wire run in the trailer.

Madge Lake had a reputation as the place to see bears feasting in their favourite dining establishment, the garbage dump. Mama Bear, Papa Bear, Baby Bear all rummaged for a free all-you-can-eat buffet meal in convivial surroundings. In the dark of the night Molly started howling like a hound pursued by bears and flung herself at the trailer door. My parents let the frenzied pup inside. The guinea pigs stayed outside, unmolested. Little Jaycie and Percy, it seemed, appealed less to bears than hundred-year-old hot dogs and other toxic waste.

Parks management had since fenced off the dump to keep bears from dining there, but other wildlife felt free to roam wherever they pleased. I stepped out of the car almost smack into a parade of mother and three baby skunks. Stripy tails held high, armed and ready, these trigger-happy characters were cute as any mammal babies could be but weren't to be messed with. I retreated a few hasty steps. Communing with skunks is best done from afar. Skunk juice was one of nature's best defences, short of claws and teeth. Anyone sprayed by a skunk could kiss their social life goodbye.

I caught a glimpse of something under the car – oh no, not the car! Not the skunks! I couldn't be sure. A raccoon had been hanging about earlier, too, making mischievous raccoon plans. Maybe it was him under the car. A camper noticed me peering under the car from a safe distance.

'If it's a skunk I'd leave it alone. If it's a raccoon, blame the raccoon moon.'

'What's that?'

'A full moon. There's one tonight. My mother calls that a raccoon moon. She says the coons get friskier than usual. Sounds like they strap sardine tins on their feet and tap dance on the trash bins.'

'Wonder what a raccoon would be doing under the car.'

'Only a raccoon knows. Probably untwizzling all your body bolts.'

The raccoon moon rose like a catapulted hub cap over the lake, into a supporting cast of celestial signal lights blinking in all directions.

The next morning Ken checked under the Chevy for signs of raccoon or skunk molestation. Finding none we drove off, expecting a good day's run through Manitoba, the most slim-waisted of the prairie provinces. There was plenty of time to trundle towards Ontario and find another pretty campground like Madge Lake before evening.

This plan failed to take into account Manitoba's lack of direct west–east roads, other than the dreaded, much-trafficked Trans-Canada Highway. Lake Manitoba and Lake Winnipeg, lying smack in the way, were to blame. In almost any other country these inland seas would win prizes for Giant Wet Thing, but they're mere puddles compared to the Great Lakes further east.

Some U-turns later, Highway 10 skewed across our path. We seized it and trundled down to Dauphin for a much-needed lunch stop. A fellow in a truck pulled in next to us.

'Say, is that a '56 Chevy? I've got a '59 Cadillac I'm restoring.' He pulled out a photo of my dream car, this time in white. I waved it meaningfully at the Beast, who turned a blind headlight and pretended not to see.

Canada is big. I'd forgotten how vastly enormous, how much sheer bigness there is. The day became dismally devoid of attractions.

'There's a dead crow,' said Ken.

'Is that an attraction?' I said. 'Shall I write that down?'

'No need to get cynical.'

At Poplarfield a Giant Roadside Deer reared up to make the day worthwhile.

It had been a disenchanting drive. The few people we did see stared as though they'd seen an alien spaceship. The Beast slunk through the towns like a kicked dog. No one called on the Cellphone That Never Rang.

'These are the sorts of places you consider yourself lucky to leave,' said Ken.

At hour thirteen of being once again on the wrong road to somewhere, I knew not where, the Beast washed up in Hnausa Beach Provincial Park on the shores of Lake Winnipeg. Like Madge Lake this was a quiet and pleasant campground despite a certain lack of luxuries like showers and loo rolls. I fell asleep to the soothing sound of small but steady surf crashing on the sandy beach of a freshwater sea.

Sleeping in the Beast was, as expected, a hundred times better than squeezing up in the Ford. For starters, Ken's feet fit inside the doors. Once we'd snapped the magnetised curtains over the windows and strung a sarong on a clothesline across the front seat, our bed was snoop-proof. The stitched headliner billowed in a pillowy white cloud. Snuggled down amongst the duvets, a light breeze blowing through the cunning anti-mozzie sleeve, we could be no more blissful in a sultan's tent.

The lack of bug life surprised and pleased me no end. On an earlier tenting trip to Manitoba mosquito death platoons had buzzed us mercilessly. How they laughed – zee zee zee! – at any attempts to smoke them out by campfire. They dive-bombed eyes and ears, bit through jeans, hair, jerseys. Their ceaseless zizzing short-circuited that piece of the human mind responsible for reminding us they're only insects and we are the masters of the planet. In full retreat I dived into the tent and stayed there, smelly and hungry. The next day I stumbled over a deer carcass. It was flat as a run-over coyote. Those bloodsucking monsters, I was sure, had got it.

Hnausa was free of death-platoon mozzies but not other small perils. In the morning I ignored a warning not to swim if a north wind was a-blowing evil bacteria this way – where was north? The perpetually north-easterly pointing compass helped not a whit. I emerged from my dip slightly cleaner but also itchier.

Gimli was next on the map. This little town of Icelanders lay straight down the road. Couldn't miss it and didn't except for a single wrong turn onto a wharf where an old gent stood next to a bucket of berley.

'What are you fishing for?'

'Fish!' barked the old gent in a succinct Scandinavian way. He pointed to two piddling perch and a sunfish. 'That's all I've got to show for six hours' fishing. Something's not right.'

I mentioned the bacteria warning sign and my early-morning dip in the lake.

'Oh, no. Something's not right.'

I itched, not wanting to think about what might not be right.

Gimli was a gorgeous wee lakeside town chock to the top of its horned helmets with Viking statues, the remains of a Viking ship buried on the shore that required some imagination to reconstruct, and signs stating 'Parking for Icelanders only'. The New Iceland Heritage museum told stories of Icelandic immigrants sleeping in tents and rotating the cat through the family beds to keep everyone warm at night. I could almost hear the Doukhobors: 'A cat! Luxury!'

Gimli had gained fame in 1983, when an Air Canada jet flying from Montréal to Edmonton ran plumb out of fuel a couple of hundred kilometres east of the town. The pilot landed the unpowered plane safely on Gimli's disused air force runway, scattering startled go-carters racing round the track on a family day out. Ground crew had loaded the first metric plane in Canada with only half the fuel it needed, following a botched imperial to metric conversion.

Perhaps the story of the Gimli Glider explained why many Canadians were so deeply, searingly mistrustful of the metric system that a simple can of beans carried not only English and French but also imperial and metric information, to cover all situations where beans might be eaten.

In a city full of Icelanders we met probably the only man who wasn't. Tyrone crewed on the $3 million Canadian Coastguard boat *Vakta*. He gladly toured us around this brand-new, full of bells and whistles vessel. These coastguarders weren't exactly on the coast. What did they do?

'Search and rescue on Lake Winnipeg, drop and retrieve buoys, cut down trees in the sightlines so people can see the buoys. The lake down here is eighteen miles wide. In winter the lake freezes five feet thick, so it's a seasonal job.'

Ken wanted to linger and drool over the boats bobbing in the marina but a drowning rain had started to fall. We made a hasty and regrettable decision to depart perhaps the nicest little town in all of Manitoba and pressed on to Winnipeg for the night's camping.

Winnipeg didn't look far away on the map, but getting there meant more of the jigs and turns we'd already had plenty of, plus starts and stops for pothole repairs and road widening. The Beast didn't mind all this stop-and-go. It started happily after every stop. But after the fourth lot of this in an hour a motorist's good humour wore thin.

'What was the name of the town we just passed?' I asked.

'Under Construction,' said Ken.

'Now who's being cynical.'

For a fair-sized city, Winnipeg provided little in the way of campgrounds. Tinkertown Family Fun Park might have had its attractions if you were eight, but we were looking to make our hit rate three nice quiet campsites in a row. Somewhere out of the wind and rain where tired travellers could rest with a glass or two of wine around a crackling fire. The new improved guidebook showed such a campground near the tiny speck of Sainte-Agathe, a few kilometres south of Winnipeg next to the Red River.

We shot onto the highway encircling the city, missed the turn-off to the Sainte-Agathe Highway by a whisker and soon discovered that motorists can drive round and round Winnipeg's outskirts without going anywhere else, ever. The Perimeter Highway eventually tired of this game and chucked us out on the road to Sainte-Agathe. There was nothing resembling a campground in the little town, but a jolly fellow in the gas and grocery store pointed across the highway.

'Der is no camping 'ere in Santagat, le camping est là.'

This abrupt slip into Frenchness, so far from Québec, reminded me that in the eighteenth century French and Métis explorers and trappers had sortied down the Winnipeg and Red Rivers. In this century their Franco-Manitobain descendants kept a tight grip on the language. Showing a certain elegant fluency I deciphered Santagat to mean Sainte-Agathe and 'le camping' to mean, well, 'le camping'. The campground, advertised somewhat damply as 'Une oasis dans la plaine', lacked any other vehicles or people except for one seemingly uninhabited RV and a silent young man at the office. While the attendant searched for a camping form and some firewood I prowled around the adjacent Flood Plain Interpretive Centre. The informative display clearly demonstrated, by photo and fact, the folly of building anything, including campgrounds, on a low broad plain where sudden floods sweep across like prairie seas. In 1997 such a flood swamped Sainte-Agathe to the rooftops. The army came to rescue townsfolk clinging to their chimneys. It was guaranteed to happen again, no one could say when.

Towards the setting sun, fat grey clouds grew fatter and greyer. Ken ripped out the grass from the corrugated-iron fire pit at our campsite. A family of eight grey mice rushed hither and thither trying to scale the corrugated iron. They finally escaped when Ken lifted up an edge and they streamed off in a grey streak towards a line of bushes.

We sipped wine sitting on the woodpile next to the fire. I felt a trifle guilty about the homeless mice, but they had many other fire pits to nest in, after all. Then the fat grey clouds opened up their bottom hatch and emptied out cold driving rain. With the flood of '97 heavy on my mind I argued for moving to higher ground or at least retreating to the Beast. But the mice had been evicted, the firewood paid for. So we sat, all alone in a treeless patch of grass on a teetery woodpile, wine in one hand and an umbrella-cum-lightning rod in the other. Rain poured in torrents down the back of necks and trousers.

The worst was yet to come. One of the little homeless mice ran up to the fire pit, threw us a tiny aggrieved scowl, and scampered off into the black and dreary night. We'd just been scolded by a mouse.

Ken does not ask for much in the way of sightseeing. A dead crow, a tree, all fine with him. But he desperately wanted to see the Beech Musketeers and de Havilland Beavers at the Western Canada Aviation Museum near Winnipeg's airport. I wanted to see the painted polar bear statues on Broadway in downtown Winnipeg. We regained the Perimeter Highway vowing to see both, in whichever order the highway allowed.

Aviation museums, like car garages, were not places I much fancied. But this one had scooped a real prize: a replica of the most fascinating piece of aeronautics ever built in the country, perhaps on the planet. The Avrocar.

The Avrocar was a genuine flying saucer. A real, silvery disc. This might explain why the good people of Poplarfield looked like they'd seen a UFO. It was designed by Briton John Frost and built during the fifties in extreme secrecy by Avro Canada. The US military, looking for disc attack weapons, took over the Avrocar project from an impatient and rapidly becoming impoverished British-Canadian venture.

The shiny silver six-metre disc looked exactly how a flying saucer should look. Pilot Spud Potocki never flew the Avrocar more than a metre or so off the ground, but it did get off the ground. In time the Americans also gave up waiting and canned Project Y. Plans for a family Avrowagon and an Avroangel air ambulance also died, alas. If they hadn't, we might all be sluicing around the skies, Jetson-like, free of wheels.

John Frost left, in what was becoming a surprisingly familiar theme, for New Zealand. He spent the rest of his days in Auckland designing clever innovations for Air New Zealand.

Avro Canada also built the world's fastest military jet at the time, the Avro Arrow, for the Canadian government. The bile of the mysterious political machinations that forced the plane to be not only grounded but destroyed still sours the craws of many a Canadian.

So what did happen, I wondered.

'The Americans killed it,' said a man with a beanbag belly sitting on a bench with his young son. 'It was faster than anything they had and they didn't like that. The Yanks don't want us to build planes of our own, they just want us to be a supply depot. Ottawa caved in to US pressure.'

There was a general muttering amongst the museum patrons. The Avro Arrow was only one bone of contention on which Canadians were forced to gnaw. What were those US military jets doing flying around their northern airspace? And why didn't American RV owners pay the twenty bucks to stay in a campground instead of squatting for free in Wal-Mart parking lots and driving honest campground owners out of business?

The teenage winner of a 1970s radio contest to complete the phrase 'As Canadian as…' summed up Canadian sentiment perfectly with her answer: 'As Canadian as possible, under the circumstances.' Still, there was much friendly feeling towards ordinary Americans. If only they'd camp where they were supposed to.

The painted polar bears on Broadway were cute and colourful but not near as thrilling as the Avrocar. Winnipeg displayed these painted polar bears for the same reason Saskatoon had painted pigs and Calgary had cows: to raise money for charity. These winsome bears gave bears everywhere a good name. As I told a scowling Ken many times, they were worth all those U-turns and driving the Beast the wrong way down narrow one-way streets and attempts to throttle each other, weren't they, mine darling.

Dawdling over bears and UFOs ate up most of the day. This left us two hundred kilometres short of the Ontario border. We broke free of the Perimeter Highway's tractor beam and headed east again to find a quiet campsite, the better to sit around a crackling fire sipping a glass or two of wine, free from condemnation by rodent.

Whiteshell Provincial Park, on the edge of the Canadian Shield, looked like a winner: rocky, laky, stunningly woodsy; and a mere stone's throw from Ontario. The road curled past lily ponds full of the flowers the Ojibwe First Nation people called 'the star fallen in the water', according to the park brochure, and lakes afloat with ululating loons. The only sites left in the entire park were in West Hawk Lake Campground.

And then it became clear why Winnipeg lacks campgrounds. The campers all came to West Hawk Lake Campground. Our campsite, D5, was trouble from the word go. No trees, not even a twig, separated our site from the packs of Winnipeg boy racers ten to a tent yowling mating calls to girl racers, blasting radios and chucking beer bottles blithely hither and yon, yon being perilously close to the Beast.

Being a teenager once counts for nothing when you're as old as a vintage car and wanting a good night's rest. It only counts at drive-in movies. This may sound like the hypocritical rantings of the grumpy middle-aged. It is. Along with the outdoorsy joys of camping came the downs – toilet blocks creepier than crime scenes, the odd noisy bunch of high-spirited fellow campers. We expected this. A pair of good ear plugs solved a great deal.

And camping came in many memorable forms, from a stoical New Zealand backpack tramp up a solitary trail lugging home, kitchen and wardrobe, to a wondrous night in a swanky Italian marble marvel peopled by the beautiful and the groomed blow-drying their moustaches. Still, I clung to the old-fashioned notion of camping as a peaceful retreat to a shrub-shrouded glen, where loons crooned and wild animals frolicked. At West Hawk Lake, the other campers *were* the wild animals.

As the night wore on the din in Teen Tentville worsened. I had visions of the two of us cracking up entirely and driving the Beast headlong into the melee, its toothy grill demonic in the campfire light, scattering the partygoers like swine before our copper-and-cream pearl. I cornered two security guards patrolling the campground and asked, politely, what could be done.

'We do our best but it's not easy. We shut one group down but after we go away they start up again.'

There was no choice but to move or murder somebody.

'This is the noisiest campground I've ever been to in either hemisphere,' I remarked to the park officer, in case they were conducting a survey. 'Can we have another site please?'

The park officer tried to soothe us with the hopeful but unlikely story that any noisy campers would be evicted.

'You'll have to evict all of D block,' I argued. 'I'll sleep in the parking lot if I have to.'

'There aren't any other tent sites, just RV sites.'

I stabbed a finger at the Beast. 'There's our car. We sleep in it.

Tonight, it's an RV.'

After whispering with another park officer she offered another site, A1.

'You'll have to be gone by three pm tomorrow, it's booked,' she said.

'We'll be gone at the crack of dawn.' I plucked the permit from her fingers and strode past a line of teenagers waiting for a tent site of their own to vandalise.

'D5 is free.' I stalked off.

This was shameful, cranky old bat behaviour, and I blush to recall it. But A1 truly was A1, lakeside and privately wooded amongst quiet RV families. Up the road some thoughtful RV neighbours had set up a giant TV screen. Ken went along to watch. I lay in the Beast's plush Arabian Nights bed lulled by a *Star Wars* soundtrack and the hhoo-*hhwweee*-hhoo of loons. A flat coyote morphed into a pleasant moose moment.

In the morning, Ken fossicked for a breakfast cookie to munch with his milky coffee.

'Aw, what!'

All the cookies, and the plastic bag, bore mouse-sized nibble marks. But the rodents' revenge didn't interest me. I itched. A Son of Evil Bacteria rash crept where no rash should ever creep.

'Your hair looks like a basting brush,' said Ken in a thoughtful attempt at distraction.

Ah, camping.

Heroes and Hell Riders

' Crazy people! Why is everyone in such a hurry? '

Alex Nilsson, endurance roller skier, near Nipigon, Ontario

Across the Ontario border the Canadian Shield's granite boulders heaved through a scurf of soil. Rusty ferns fringed a boreal forest dense and dark with balsam fir, black spruce and red pine. This was Precambrian country, at least 500 million years old and undeservedly uglified along the length of the highway by billboards advertising new kitchens, real estate and supermarkets, and signs advertising signs.

We'd met up with the Trans-Canada Highway. In this part of Ontario it disguised itself as Highway 17 but it didn't fool me. It was the only road into Northern Ontario from western Canada so we were stuck on it, just us and all the other Ontario–Manitoba traffic and dozens of big, big semi-trailer trucks in a big, big hurry.

Until now other drivers had mostly been kind. Showing respect for the Beast's age and lack of speediness, passing drivers gave us room to manoeuvre. Most drivers waved and grinned as they flashed their rear bumpers. Ken did his best to keep up to the speed limit and tried to pull over even on thin shoulders to let faster traffic pass.

Truck drivers in Ontario did not care. They had loads to haul, schedules to stick to and bosses to keep happy. They chivvied and menaced the poor Beast so badly it shuddered each time one of these nightmares-on-wheels roared by. Fearsome metal jaws surrounding the trucks' massive grilles gave them the predatory look of great white sharks bearing down upon a baby seal.

Kenora was a comforting place to stop, draw a trembling breath and take a walk along the Lake of the Woods. A Chevy lover who'd spotted the for sale sign followed the car into the car park.

'Is that a '55 Chevy? I drove a '59 Ford to California once.'

Ken chatted away for a pleasant half hour about the Beast's

best features, notably the new non-leaky transmission. I sat on a bench by the lake trying to retrieve a message from an unfamiliar Manitoba number on the Cellphone That Never Rang. I was certain we'd hooked a Beast-buying fish. But neither of us had any luck. The Chevy lover didn't love it enough to part with any money. The woods blocked cellphone reception completely, a problem I hadn't fully considered when I hatched the master plan. Nor had I divined that, in the event of a Beast versus truck crash, any survivors dragging their crushed and bloodied bodies towards the cellphone to get help would be miserably disappointed.

It seemed like this might happen sooner rather than later. Near Vermilion Bay a semi-trailer charging down a hill lost traction rounding a curve. The truck skewed sideways like a white wall of death for three horrible seconds before slewing back across the centre line.

'These are worse than the terrible Tata trucks of India,' said Ken, unhooking his fingernails from the steering wheel.

On our motorcycle ride through Rajasthan a few years earlier the terrible Tata trucks had not been a bikie's friend. They drove the wrong way on divided highways. One passed a car passing us passing a camel wagon on a country road. They routinely tipped over, spilling motorcycle-wrecking bags of rice or bricks onto the road. This felt the same, without the camel wagons and rice.

Needing another little break, Ken diverted off track at Ignace for a nostalgic tour of the town and the nearby railway yard. In the summer before I met him seventeen-year-old Ken and his fifteen-year-old friend Terry set out to hitchhike three thousand kilometres from Saskatoon to Toronto. They packed thirty-five dollars each, some cans of beans and a few chocolate bars. For several days all went as well as can be expected for a pair of unwashed hitchhiking teenagers. But at Ignace things came to a halt. The boys sat on the roadside for two days in blistering heat. Cars passed them, stopped, then took off as soon as they laid hand on door handle.

On day three a sympathetic Ignace resident invited them to his house for a cold beer. The fridge contained, besides a whole lot of beer, a lone curled-up fish. He gave them each a beer then insisted they admire the cut on his head where his wife had whacked him over the head with a bottle. As they peered at the gory wound the head-whacking wife charged into the room brandishing a large butcher knife. Threatening to slice the lot of them into salami she chased the teenagers out of the house. That night they slept in the ruts of an abandoned road.

Ignace having lost its charm, the boys noticed an awful lot of freight trains shuttling through the town. They traded their hitchhiking thumbs for a stint of freight-hopping like regular hobos through Ontario all the way to Toronto. An awful lot of freight trains still shuttled through the town. I tossed around the notion of putting the Beast on a train transporter to Toronto and us on a nice comfy berth. But that would be cheating and cowardly, and far too sensible.

'Ignace looks a lot more built up,' said Ken, trawling past a short strip of houses and three petrol stations. He pulled into a truck stop to fill up. I sneaked over to have a look at the enemy.

The truck driver leaning on a rig named 'Black Fang' or some such took a drag on his cigarette. 'Somethin' I can help ya with?'

'Oh no. Just having a look.' Then, stupidly, 'You guys go pretty fast down these roads.'

He sucked another drag. 'You a cop or somethin'?'

'No.'

'Company spy guys?'

'No, no.' This wasn't going well at all. 'We're driving an old car and we have to stick to the speed limit. It doesn't go that fast.'

I nodded at the Beast in a pathetic play for pity. The trucker glanced over, snorted and ground the cigarette under his boot heel. 'Piece a' advice, ma'am. Get movin' or get outta the road.'

The signs advertising bargain whiteware dribbled away to more agreeable entertainments: cartoonish moose-warning signs and whimsical hay-bale figures dressed up in aprons.

At Kakabeka Falls the fair had come to town. Eating candy apples and peperoni pizza by the slice, watching people staggering off the Stomach-Churner or the Brain-Banger trying to keep *their* candy apples and peperoni pizza inside where it belonged, all in all, good fun. Back at the Beast two cheerful beer swillers left over from a rock concert swayed in appreciative unison. Both clutched a can in each hand.

'Nice car, eh. You shoulda bin here a coupla hours earlier, before it rained, the town was packed, eh,' said partygoer number one.

'Packed, eh,' agreed his friend.

'Is that right?' Ken looked around at the few folk lingering in the streets. 'Where are they all staying?'

'Wherever they fall down, eh,' shrugged partygoer number one.

'Yah, eh,' agreed his friend.

At Thunder Bay stood a statue of one of Canada's most beloved figures. Not a war veteran, not a politician, not even a beaver, but Terry Fox. A quarter-century ago Terry, a curly-headed twenty-one-year-old from British Columbia with one good leg and one prosthetic one, wetted a foot in the Atlantic Ocean in Newfoundland and started running west. His goal: to run clear across Canada in a Marathon of Hope, raising money for cancer research. I remembered this very well. The whole of the country followed him step by painful step. He pounded out more than five thousand kilometres before a cancer relapse forced him off the road near Thunder Bay. When he died the following year an entire country mourned. Heroes don't grow on trees.

Along the eighty kilometres of the Terry Fox Courage Highway east of Thunder Bay, other determined characters struggled on their own missions. A keen cyclist strapped into a recliner bike pedalling up a hill passed a pair of hitchhikers and a panting hitchhiking dog. We uncharitably passed them all. I felt sorry for the hitchhikers and their dog. But short of strapping them to the roof or stuffing them in front of the engine there wasn't room for any more bags, dogs or people in the Beast. They looked up briefly, beseechingly, then plodded on to wherever they were going. If they had any sense, it would be the nearest rail yard.

Near Nipigon a sign on a parked RV simply said, 'Skier on the road'. This was summer. What the hey? A lone figure striding over the next rise solved the mystery. Alex Nilsson set out from Creston in British Columbia to roller ski across Canada and raise funds for diabetes research, in the Terry Fox tradition. He was an endurance sports virtuoso. He was seventy years old.

Each ski rolled along on four small inflatable wheels – if he got a flat he'd have to patch it like a bicycle tyre. Highway rules allowed him to ski only on the skinny gravel shoulder, but he rocketed along at ten kilometres per hour, covering about seventy kilometres each day on tyre-testing roads with traffic hurtling along not a metre from his poles.

He shared our opinion about the traffic. 'Crazy people! Why is everyone in such a hurry?'

He too was Newfoundland-bound. 'I'll see you there in September!'

Such admirable optimism. The shoulder shrank to a measly line of gravel barely navigable by squirrels never mind roller skiers. The ditch crumbled away to unforgiving boulders. I hoped Alex had a guardian angel riding heavenly shotgun on his shoulder.

Only a few minutes later a trucker honked for us to pull over. Impossible. The shoulder hadn't got any bigger, nor the roadside rocks smaller. The trucker honked again. We couldn't move an inch. The trucker swerved out, missed the car by the width of a chrome strip and cut in front of us, close, very, very close. A Saskatchewan licence plate adorned the bumper which, if it came any closer, I'd be wearing on my forehead.

Ken braked. The Beast hit a bump. Went airborne. Bounced hard on its elderly suspension. Skidded sideways towards the rocks. Crockery and cutlery and cans rattled and clattered in the back. Into that weightless moment came one clear thought: Mom's first rule of travel. The food wasn't in covered bins. If a crash didn't knock us unconscious a flying can of beans surely would.

With skill born from an adolescence spent doing doughnuts on gravel roads, Ken grappled the Beast back onto the asphalt. 'BASTARD!' he bellowed.

'That crazy trucker's from Saskatchewan!' Huff puff. I was outraged. It wasn't very neighbourly. 'I'm sorry I didn't get his licence number.' More self-righteous huff, puffs.

Ken planted his foot on the pedal. The Beast's engine roared. Steadily we gained on the truck. Sixty miles an hour, seventy, eighty—

Good gawd. They were both crazy.

Ninety miles an hour—

I cracked.

'What are you doing! This is an old car! We are going to blow the motor and die!'

'You wanted his licence number. There it is. Write it down.'

I wrote it down. Another flat coyote to add to the pack.

The Lonesome Highway, Part II

' Thought I'd never get outta there. '

Tim, hitchhiker, near Wawa, Ontario

The map of Ontario fans out across the Beast's bench seat. It takes up the whole space.

'Where are we?' asks Ken.

'Here.' I point to a speck not half way through the province. Then I fold up the map so only part of it shows. It's healthier that way.

The Beast senses this yawning emptiness is not the place to act up. It doesn't. We drive past rocks and trees, trees and rocks, fields, fields, fields. It's now clear why truckers hurry to put this space behind them. I squeeze out a drop of sympathy.

But here comes a roadside attraction. At White River a giant wooden thermometer flanked by an eskimo and an igloo reads -72°F (-58°C), to back the town's claim to be the coldest place in Canada. This is almighty, tooth-crackingly cold; cold enough to freeze spit and the lips that make it. There's another giant thermometer at the other end of town, just in case visitors miss the message the first time.

White River is not the coldest place in Canada. Cold is cold – it seems churlish to quibble – but the tiny settlement of Snag in the Yukon holds the record for all of North America at -81°F (-63°C). Record for the Northern Hemisphere: -90°F (-68°C) in Verkhoyansk, Russia. Record for the whole of the planet: -129°F (-89°C) at Vostok, the Russian science station in Antarctica. Record for the universe: some day someone will come down in an Avrocar and tell us.

Not content with only one claim to fame, White River has two. Winnie the Pooh was born here. A lieutenant from Winnipeg passing through the town during World War II paid a hunter a small sum for a small black bear cub he named Winnie, after his home town. The lieutenant took Winnie to England as the brigade mascot, but when the troops trekked off to France, the London Zoo billeted Winnie. A certain A. A. Milne and his son Christopher Robin visited her often. The Pooh statue at White River is sweet, a bear in a tree framed by summer marigolds.

We point south again. The journey takes on an airless beinglessness. This must be what it's like in space. The day trickles by in treacle time.

'Are we there yet?' says the navigator.

'Are we there yet?' says the driver.

At Wawa a svelte giant goose overlooks the town, whose name means 'wild goose' in the Ojibwe tongue. Highway 101 lures us on to Timmins for a gander at the Shania Twain Centre, but an oversized water fowl wins over a shrine to a country rocker every time. Near Wawa a young hitchhiker stands thumb out, pack on back. I look at Ken. He whistles a few bars of 'Killer on the Road'.

'That could've been you,' I remind him.

'Where will we put him?'

'He's not that big. He can lie down in the back. He can entertain us.'

The young hitchhiker tosses his pack in the back and crawls in.

'Thanks. I've been standing there a while. Thought I'd never get outta there.'

'I know what you mean,' says Ken, ready to swap rollicking stories from on the road.

The young hitchhiker says his name is Tim. Then he falls asleep on the Beast's comfy bed. He utters not one more word until we let him out at Lake Superior Provincial Park, on the shores of Gitchee Gumee, 'kitchi-gummi' as the Ojibwe called it, 'great lake.' Then he says, 'Wow. That's a big lake.'

And so it is. Lake Superior is the largest freshwater lake on this earth. Storms blow up and sink ships to the bottom of its four-hundred-metre depths. The ore carrier *Edmund Fitzgerald*, made infamous by Canadian balladeer Gordon Lightfoot's song 'Wreck of the Edmund Fitzgerald', foundered in this lake thirty years ago. All hands were lost. None has ever been recovered.

It's also mistily, surpassingly beautiful, encircled by the sort of mossy hollows and bogs a couple of moose would book for their honeymoon.

Southern Ontario draws nearer. Sault Ste. Marie, a short bridge across the border from Michigan, is the home town of Canada's first astronaut and the world's first female astronaut, Roberta Bondar. So says a giant roadside sign. There are no giant roadside Robertas.

Sault Ste. Marie is the first place in Northern Ontario to beam out a cellphone signal strong enough to retrieve the Manitoba Beast buyer's voicemail message. It's taken a few days but hopes are high he's still interested. The voice from Manitoba says, 'You're carrying a lot of baggage. You need maximum psi. Put some air in your tires.'

The Beast deserved a little break. The old car had done its best to keep us safe in the face of truck terrorism. The new transmission performed flawlessly. If you can't beat 'em, join 'em, it seemed to have decided. No point being hauled kicking and spitting parts the whole way across the country. It behaved so well I felt bad about the ad on its window branding it as a Beast for sale and so unwanted and, worse, unloved.

The map showed a car ferry, the MS *Chi-Cheemaun* ('big canoe' for those still learning Ojibwe), that crossed the next Great Lake, Huron, from South Baymouth at the tip of Manitoulin Island to Tobermory on the Bruce Peninsula. The ferry was our ticket off the snarly Trans-Canada Highway. We pootled across the island in a state of joy. On board the boat we left the Beast below decks to swap stories with the RVs and SUVs and went off in search of entertainment.

One of the crew, Old Brian, was a salty seaman from Cape Breton in Nova Scotia. He did a bit of everything on the boat, including 'public relations'.

'I can tell you stories,' he said, 'just don't believe a bit of 'em.'

Old Brian was the son of a miner, one of five children. 'That's small for Cape Breton, there's usually eighteen or twenty.' He'd sailed all his life, on tugs on Vancouver Island, on ocean-going vessels out of Halifax. On a trip from Ireland sailing for Newfoundland a wrecking storm blew up off the Azores. 'The ship came down the waves like an elevator, five fishing boats went down that night. I got off that boat and quit the job on the spot.'

Now he sailed the Great Lakes, but his home and his heart were in North Sydney on Cape Breton Island. 'The lake is as deep as the mountains are high. My neighbour plays "Amazing Grace" on the bagpipes, it echoes off the highlands and makes your hair stand on end.' I put Cape Breton on the list of places to see on the trip, minus the bagpipes.

Up in the wheelhouse first mate Terry, and Dave the relief helmsman, watched the radar guiding the big canoe over the flat glittering lake. 'Sometimes the gales blow ten- or fifteen-metre waves over the bow,' said Terry. 'The radar goes to ninety-six miles so you can see a storm coming.'

Dave let me take the wheel. Brave man. He didn't know about the gear-shifting incident near Kamsack, and I wasn't telling. I piloted the largest ferry plying the Great Lakes for a full five minutes without incident.

Southern Ontarians lived along the yellow brick road. The south was handsome with cornfields and goldenrod, elegant with porticoed Georgian brick houses as old as the money that built them. The comely city of Stratford, reclining along the Avon River was, not surprisingly, home to the Stratford Shakespearean Festival and, perhaps a little more surprisingly, the Ontario Pork Congress.

As Ken steered the Beast into a car park so we could stroll upon the banks of the Avon, a young man stopped to ask about the price of the car. He'd been out walking his wee son in a buggy. A young daughter loitered nearby. While he and Ken chatted about valves and revved the engine, the better to see the Beast rock with that V8 torque, the young daughter in charge of the buggy seized the opportunity to rid herself of the competition. She let the buggy go. It whizzed down the footpath. As it neared the kerb and ugly disaster an elderly lady snatched the handle, hauling the buggy to a stop with all her strength. The young dad was so fully aghast to have nearly disposed of his first-born son while talking cars he scarpered without another word.

Funambulists, Fetishes and Felines

' Please put a gold coin in the tin for the Old Ponies' retirement fund. '

Pony Boy, harness fetishist, Toronto, Ontario

Niagara Falls, said my guidebook, was one of the most visited places in Canada. That sounded like an excellent reason to avoid it like a rampant contagious disease. Twelve million people flocked to the honeymoon capital of the world every year to slurp ice cream, scare themselves witless at the ghost houses and drink bubbly in heart-shaped spa pools. And maybe fit in a little squiz at the two sets of famous falls.

But we had to go. It was our duty as Canadian citizens, albeit lapsed ones, to see what people from all over the world came to see. I braced myself for one of those horrible disappointments in life your mother warned you about, like spending your hard-earned allowance on a 'ruby' ring then getting a piece of junk so obviously fake you're forced to trade it profitably to your pal from the trailer court.

I navigated without incident down Lundy's Lane on the outskirts of Niagara Falls. Lundy's Lane had been the site of a bloody battle (between Americans intent on invading Canada and the British Empire intent on hanging on to it) in the War of 1812, naturally still being fought in 1814. A colony of campgrounds on the very plain where the battle took place memorialised the hundreds of troops who died. Ken tucked the Beast into a quiet family campground across from the gentlemen's establishment of Seductions, where we caught the shuttle bus to Clifton Hill and all the other action.

Niagara Falls was a true delight. Tourists would be hard pressed to find the equal of its cheerful unmitigated bunkum, tat, frippery and funhouse yuk-yuks elsewhere in Canada. Happy crowds – more post-honeymooners with kids than dewy-eyed newlyweds – surged up and down Clifton Hill enjoyably frittering away their hard-earned money on the Ripley's Believe It or Not Museum

(King Kong chest-thumping atop it); the House of Frankenstein; House of Dracula; Louis Tussaud's English Wax Museum (which started it all nearly fifty years ago) and three more wax museums of its ilk; the Guinness World Records hall – see footage of the man with thousands of bees on his face and people who can make their eyes bug out of their sockets! – numerous spook-and-ghoul houses; games of chance; trick mirrors; having their photos taken on a Harley; eating hot dogs, pizza, burgers, fantasy fudge on the street or meals at a rainforest café with live sharks swimming in a tank; buying 'I survived Niagara Falls' T-shirts and motorised hats and Pink Panther slippers. We took each other's photos in a fat suit and toasted the sheer nerve of the place with warm beer in a plastic cup.

At the bottom of Clifton Hill the American Falls and Canada's Horseshoe Falls competed for the prize for most spectacular Giant Natural Thing. Rainbows – real ones – wavered in the spray flung from the thundering colossus wetting all the falls watchers on the Maid of the Mist boats.

'Isn't it amazing,' said a chubby fellow in a Kansas City T-shirt leaning on the rail beside me. 'No matter what happens, they don't turn off. They pour all day, all night long, whether we're watching or not.'

Some folk weren't content to watch. In 1859 French funambulist Charles Blondin walked a three-inch thick tightrope over the Niagara Falls gorge. The next year he cooked an omelette up there, skipped along the rope on stilts, and walked it blindfolded, in a sack and carrying his manager. School teacher Annie Taylor surfed the fifty-three-metre Horseshoe Falls in a barrel in 1901. Others attempting the same by jet ski or kayak have died a wet and wretched death. I watched a tiny figure walk a tightrope between the Skylon Tower and the Casino Niagara. Would he fall? Was he real? Was anything real in this town? Maybe the falls themselves were only a hologram.

Every kind of tourist promenaded up and down the waterfront filling up the memory cards of their digital cameras. Indian women swathed in saris, Tibetan monks swathed in saffron robes, Italian honeymooners swathed in each other. Large North Americans in small shorts, a clutch of giggly teenage girls in silly hats, Mexican cowboys in chinstrap sombreros.

At dusk, coloured lights played pink and green on the falls like liquid aurora borealis. The shuttle bus ferried us back to the campground, to the Beast waiting quietly under an elm tree, and to the 'Girls Girls Girls' sign at Seductions playing pink and purple like neon aurora borealis.

Friends in Toronto had invited us to visit them in their Cabbagetown home. Keen to spend a few days with familiar faces and sleep in a bed lacking wheels, although not so keen to navigate into Toronto, I phoned for directions. We left Niagara Falls on the QEW.

The Queen Mother didn't deserve the madly trafficked Queen Elizabeth Way, the eight-lane expressway to Toronto, as a namesake. The Beast, I suspected, had never set tyre amongst such a honking milieu of breakneck speedsters in the whole of its fifty years. Showing a fine sense of self-preservation and, perhaps, sniffing a chance to rest in friendly territory for a few days, it bunched up its haunches and sprang forward in true thoroughbred style. We shot straight to the beating heart of Toronto.

Niagara Falls had jolted us back into the land of cities, or a fantasyland version of one. Toronto slapped us about the cheeks, shouted, 'You've hit the big time now, ya mongrels!' and pitched us into the hubris of Canada's largest metropolis. True confession: Toronto's Lester B. Pearson International Airport was the closest I'd ever been to the city itself. In nearly thirty years of living in Canada, I always turned west to Vancouver or Calgary for a big-city fix, never east to Toronto. Ken had not set foot in Toronto since his thwarted hitchhiking trip.

At a set of lights on Wellesley Street a bearded fellow in a deerskin loin cloth and a hair shirt hollered, 'Love your car! She's a honey!' I liked the place already. Ken liked the rumble of the dual exhaust bouncing off the first high-rise buildings we'd seen for some time.

In the nineteenth century, Cabbagetown residents had planted a bounty of brassicas in the front gardens of their brownstone houses. These lovely homes were now cabbageless, save for the flags festooned with the round green veggies flying from gateposts.

Our Cabbagetown friends wined us and dined us in unparalleled style. We strolled down to Kensington's old and funky markets full of fragrant cheese warehouses stuffed to the rafters with fromages ferreted from every part of the globe, disappointing Portuguese fishmongers hopefully hefting glossy-eyed tuna.

Out of streets full of eateries, Café la Gaffe on Baldwin Street promised crème brûlée made to French impressionist Claude Monet's own recipe. This was taking a little risk: the café's name loosely translated as 'Café by Mistake'. It wasn't a mistake. Indeed, said the waiter, the luscious crème brûlée was Monet's own, resurrected from his cooking journals. We'd visited Monet's vast and elegant gardens in Giverny on the European trip, and admired his paintings. When did the man find time to cook?

Next, on to Chinatown, where old ladies chopped bok choy on the pavement, a veggie seller rested inside an empty veggie bin, stacks of dried prawns, tiny to colossal, anointed the streets with the same mysterious-sea-creatures-stir-fried-in-kelp smell of Chinatowns everywhere.

On Fort Street we paused for a fortifying cup of tea. I needed all the fortifying I could get. There was one thing I really wanted to do in Toronto, even more than eating fabulous French impressionist crème brûlée.

The Toronto School of Circus Arts taught a drop-in trapeze class to all would-be trapeze artists, young or old, fit or fat, on Friday evenings. Fit or fat, I desperately wanted to go.

More true confessions: I don't like heights. Standing close to the edge of anything higher than a footpath gives me vertigo, that almost irresistible urge to fling oneself off whatever one is standing on, to end the suspense of not knowing when plummeting doom might come. Ken loves heights. When not hanging his toes over crumbling cliffs he scampers across rooftops as nonchalantly as Blondin walking his tightrope. After years of begging him, without success, to 'Please get off, down, away from there, you're going to kill yourself!' I now just make sure he is fully insured and I have the car keys.

But for me the flying trapeze class was a must. Blame Les Arts Sauts, the French trapeze company I'd seen at Wellington's International Festival of the Arts. Lying back on a deck chair oohing and aaahing as the trapeze artists swung back and forth I vowed that if I ever got the chance to fly through the air with the greatest of ease, I would.

After the tea we set off to walk. It started to rain. Then it really, really rained. We sloshed through a Niagara Falls-like deluge, slipped in pond-sized puddles and slithered soggy and dripping into what was once the *Globe and Mail* newspaper's press hall. I dried myself off with a tissue, noticing with no small trepidation the ropes and silks and wires hanging from the high ceilings. There was even a low-level practice tightrope for future funambulists. Of all of these, the flying trapeze looked the most terrifying.

Instructor Jen gathered up the five of us who'd paid our twenty-five bucks to have a go. Shawn and Cyn had the lean and flexible look of circus performers but claimed never to have attempted flying trapeze. I didn't believe it for a minute. Shawn's brother Ryan was only in town visiting but got roped into trying it himself. So did Amanda, who'd come along to watch. Jen took us through the knee hang manoeuvre on the practice bar only a few feet off the ground. Clapping a belt round each waist she showed us how to hook onto the safety line leading up the ladder. We practised bunny hops on the mats. And then it was time.

Shawn went first. As expected from an undercover circus performer he hung, swung and flung like a pro. Ryan went next. He started well, but lost momentum or possibly stomach muscles and landed heavy as a sack of spuds in the net.

A moment of doubt seized me. 'Is this the stupidest thing I've ever done?'

'Not likely,' said Ken.

Heartened, I stepped up.

'Here, let me help you clip on the safety line,' offered Adam, who controlled the safety lines from below. 'Up you go. When you're ready.'

A moment passed. Then another.

'When you're ready,' Adam encouraged.

The narrow steel ladder flexed with every step. I hadn't signed up to ride a bucking snake. I looked down. Bad mistake.

'You can do it,' called Adam.

Gawd.

'Welcome to my office,' cried the cheerful Jen at the top. 'It's only one foot by eight feet but it's cosy. Nice view from forty feet up, too.'

All I heard was 'forty feet up'. It sounded like thirty-eight feet too many.

'Stand here, hang onto the bar, arms straight. When I say hep, you bunny hop off. Are you ready?'

I twitched. Jen interpreted that to mean yes.

She called, 'Karen, knee hang, hep!'

I bunny hopped. Not quite. My knees collapsed and I fell off. Someone very close to me screamed a lung-rattling cry.

On the floor Adam called, 'Knees up!'

Knees, yes, right, the bendy bit of the leg. I aimed them at the gap, barked my shins on the bar, stuffed legs through.

Then, 'Hands off!'

Hands. Off. Wholly unnatural. But there I was, hanging upside-down, swinging through the air, flying, if more in the manner of laundry flapping on a line than a seasoned trapeze artist.

Onto the next hard thing, the back flip. I struggled to get my head around what was needed. Upside down is not a natural thinking position, except for bats.

'Just listen to what I tell you to do and then do it. Don't try to figure it out, it'll just happen,' said the patient and ridiculously confident Adam.

I let hands go, brought knees up and, against all odds, did a back flip into the net. Huzzah!

Playing at being in the circus tired body and mind. Ryan and Amanda crept away to nurse their bruises. Jen showed the three of us remaining one last trick. My blood-flooded brain wouldn't listen.

'Just let go and fly like Superman,' said Cyn.

I let go and flew like a frog.

Regaining control of some of the larger muscle groups and with a modicum of dignity I wobbled off, declining any more offers to fly like a superhero. The next day, and the next, and for an entire week, my arms punished me for punishing them. They wouldn't move. My knees looked like they'd been beaten with a bag of oranges. The bruises took two weeks to heal, the net burn on my chin took one. But if my arms had worked I'd have packed my bag and run away to join the circus. Even frogs might fly.

'Toronto is the centre of the universe,' Terry remarked during an afternoon-long liquid lunch. This was the same freight-hopping Terry who years later returned to Toronto by more conventional means, and stayed.

As we strolled from café to café, Toronto did have a 'capital of the urban cosmos' feel, though a fellow in a floppy purple bonnet babbling into a popsicle-stick cellphone seemed just as much a citizen as luncheoners talking stocks on hands-free Motorolas.

Back in Cabbagetown many of the world's nationalities gathered for a go at their share of the city's riches. At a small flea market Senegalese trinket-sellers, Indian cloth merchants, and an Afghani carpet pedlar spilling carpets out of a supermarket trolley peaceably flogged their wares.

'How long have you been in Toronto?' I asked the carpet seller.

'Long, long time.' He rolled a mournful eye. 'Afghanistan, my home. Cannot go back. But this is good place for everybody.'

At the Fetish Fair on Church Street the fetish community flogged, well, themselves. In the stiflingly hot sweaty weather buttocks rose like furred dough through seatless leather trousers. Street stalls did a brisk trade in whips and chains. A slim young man strapped from fetlock to forelock in horse harness, bit under his chin, trotted down the road pulling weary fair goers in a chariot. Pony Boy posed like a pro for photos.

'Please put a gold coin in the tin for the Old Ponies' retirement fund,' he whickered, tossing his tawny mane in the direction of a tin in the chariot. So I did. The knacker's yard would be a sad end for Pony Boy.

The fair was disappointingly short on shoes, feathers and other such fetishist objects, although the boot-black stall did a thumping trade. Still, the day was young – the lycrawear contest didn't start until dusk. But our lazy days in the centre of the universe were over. Time to move on to the next stop, the nation's capital, and a date with some cats.

Highway 401 had a reputation for striking fear and loathing into visiting motorists. It was more frightening than the QEW. We bailed out onto the slower Highway 7 – which turned out to be once again the sneaky Trans-Canada masquerading as something else – hurried through Toronto's Stepford-like bedroom communities and burst into the countryside. For a time we ambled pleasantly amongst the cornfields and huts selling corn, blueberry huts selling jam and fresh berries and spud huts selling French fries, before giving in and stopping for corn and blueberries and fries to fortify ourselves for a foray into another city.

Ottawa was the type of big city you could live in and fool yourself into thinking it wasn't a big city. Built along the Ottawa River, the city is so greenly lush, so winningly handsome it deserves to be the nation's capital. Queen Victoria chose Ottawa over such glamour pusses as Toronto, Montréal and Québec City. They'd been in a snit ever since, but it was one of the old gal's better decisions.

We strolled up Parliament Hill past statues of the nation's prime ministers. Sir John A. Macdonald, the very first. John George Diefenbaker, number thirteen, a Saskatoon native son done good. Grumpy William Lyon Mackenzie King, who held office for twenty-two years, helped along by tea-leaf readings and seances with his deceased mother. The strain showed.

Each of these past politicians wore a jaunty toupée of pigeon poop. Why people thought statues were a good and decent monument to good and decent men was a mystery. They almost always ended up wearing pigeon-poop toupées. No pigeon, though, had pooped on Terry Fox in Thunder Bay. Pigeons, like skunks, had their say in the only way they know how.

The stone parliament buildings exuded such gothic grandeur we just knew there were important things going on in there. But we passed up the chance to tour the place. There were more interesting goings-on in a shadow parliament behind the real thing, where twenty-odd calico, ginger and tabby cats lived in two miniature plywood houses caregiver René Chartrand had built to resemble the parliament buildings. The cats shared their digs with ambitious squirrels and groundhogs.

René hadn't missed a day's cat feeding since he started, but we arrived too early for the four o'clock session. Fill-in cat feeder Christ Oliver sat on a bench near the mini-parliament. Four fat cats sat on him. Oliver fed cat treats to the cats and squirrel treats to the squirrels. The squirrels wanted the cat treats. The cats wanted the squirrels to bug off. A skirmish broke out on his knees. When not feeding cats, shaggy-haired serious Oliver wrote and illustrated graphic novels. He showed me one. His exquisite illustrations featured Wonder Woman-proportioned catwomen getting into messes around Ottawa. At least that was my guess: the book was all in French.

I patted a couple of the cats. These were very lucky cats, living rent-free on some of the country's priciest real estate. The human parliament's tolerance for a bunch of stray felines hinted that, whatever the Ottawa politicians' faults, they couldn't be all bad.

The next best thing on Parliament Hill was the Royal Canadian Mounted Police. At the Peace Tower in front of parliament, one of these red-jacketed knights of the realm posed tirelessly for photos of kids and tourists patting the horse. I took my turn for a pose with the Mountie. Who wouldn't? Mounties, like maple leaves, beavers and moose, like loons and loonies, are a potent Canadian symbol. A friend in New Zealand once dreamt of being a Mountie, but the closest he got was wearing a Mountie costume at our Canadian editor-in-chief's farewell party in Auckland. I got to wear a gopher suit and to smack the editor-in-chief in the face with a banana cream pie. Dreams do come true.

Sareb the Mountie and Linus the horse were not actors. They were the real thing. Talk, dark and handsome, both were beautifully behaved and polished till they shone. I could see my reflection in Sareb's brown knee-high boot. Linus tolerated prods and pokes while Sareb politely steered the curious away from the business end of the horse.

Taking a short cut across a car park a bit later we stumbled onto the Mounties' temporary stables. Sareb sat under a tree, unfrocked and sipping a cup of coffee.

'Hey, go behind the shed, we have visitors,' Sareb called to a fellow Mountie peeling off his trousers.

Linus, said Sareb, was thirteen years old, only half the age of the oldest horse. Sareb and Linus had just finished their one-hour shift standing outside parliament for photo ops. The horses took a rest in their stables. The Mounties took off their tunics and mucked out stalls. Behind the scenes at the Mounties didn't smell terribly glamorous. But besides doing photo ops Sareb and Linus rode in the RCMP Musical Ride. This was not your average travelling pony show; the Musical Ride *was* glamorous. It was a show to stir the pride of Canadians, no matter where they found themselves.

I'd seen it once in a small northern Manitoba town. The horses gleamed as dark as burnished ebony and the scarlet Mounties sat tall in a row, sun striking gold off brass buttons. They cantered into the grounds, red-and-white pennons flying. Dust flew from hooves. For an exhilarating hour, thirty-two horses and riders spun and wheeled and turned through the thread the needle, the wagon wheel and the thrilling grand finale, the galloping lancer charge. At the end, the MC asked the crowd to please rise for the singing of 'O Canada'.

'Old Canada!' squealed a preschool tot behind me.

The Musical Ride did that. It made Canadians large and small, lapsed or not, stand up and squeal for Old Canada.

The French Connection

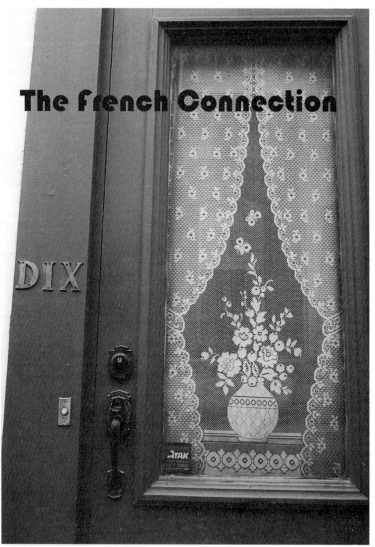

DIX

' C'est magnifique! '

Classic-car lovers everywhere, Québec

The province of Québec lay just across the river from Ottawa. After a few false starts – 'It's this way!' 'No it's that way! I can see the blimmin' bridge!' – we crossed over to Gatineau's modest suburbs, and total French immersion.

'Meubles à vendre, tracteur à louer,' I chanted, practising for those occasions when I needed to buy furniture or hire a tractor. 'Arrêt! Stop!' I howled at a railway crossing.

'I know that one,' said Ken.

On our first road trip to the east decades earlier, Québec quirked her pinky finger. We fell in love. People actually lived like this – laughing, drinking, eating outdoors? There was wine for sale in campground shops. Wine in campgrounds! Inconceivable.

Saskatoon started life as a temperance colony, a teetotal haven from the evils of drink. In the not too distant past, to buy a bottle of liquor a thirsty Saskatonian entered the government-run liquor board store, wrote their request on a slip of paper and handed it to the sepulchral attendant guarding the counter, who assessed age and troublemaking potential. If the customer passed the test the attendant withdrew to some locked-down dungeon in the back to fetch the hard-won bottle. Whether the government feared an unending drunken frenzy of folk seizing bottles off shelves and guzzling them on the spot, or a plague of shifty-eyed shoplifters bootlegging the stuff in Kinsman Park, was hard to say. Whatever, it made innocent booze-buyers feel Oliver Twisty: Please sir, may I have some more? Québec treated grown-ups like grown-ups.

Other than the French signs and freely accessible booze there was another clue that we'd crossed into Québec. Crosses with or without Jesus on them loomed everywhere: in people's gardens, in roadside rest areas. This was Catholic country, where the devout weren't afraid to show it.

In the village of Papineauville I thought I saw a vision.

'Turn! Go back! You have to see this!'

Well used to doing U-turns, often for precious little reward, Ken patiently found a driveway, backed in, reversed and set off down the way we'd come. 'What are we looking for?'

'Well, it's a...I don't know how to explain it – there!'

'There' was half an old car. Half a fifties Mercury car, painted exactly like the Beast, hanging high on a garage wall. This was quite the find. It reminded the Beast that well-behaved cars earned a thrilling life on the road while badly behaved cars got split down the middle and trophied like a trout on somebody's wall. As we admired this piece of ingenuity a car drove up and two raffish characters got out. The driver, whom I took to be the garage owner, called out something in French. This sounded like 'Get off my land' but actually was 'Do you want to trade?', as he eventually said in English. He pointed at the Beast and then the half Merc.

'Eet's missing on four cylinders. Ha ha! Your car, c'est magnifique.'

The previous owner had frescoed up the Merc in this fashion. The headlights and indicators still worked. Did it improve business? Our new friend couldn't say, 'but people dey know where de garage, she is'.

I could see Ken trying to work out how to mount an entire motorcycle on our living-room wall. I lured him back into the car with promises of chocolate before he could glean any hot tips on wall fastenings.

The town of Lachute held a *marché aux puces* – a flea market – on Tuesdays and Saturdays. This was Tuesday. By the look of the traffic snarling up the main street it was a popular event, even midweek. Down a back lane locals rented out their front lawns and driveways as parking, for two loonies, or one toonie, a car. Two elderly gents in easy chairs gestured the Beast into a spot beneath the trees.

'Move over, you should make room for anudder car,' cried one, intent on pinching the most profit from this parking empire. His wife scolded him in French. 'It is OK, you can stay there.'

left **Toronto, Ontario** What's she smiling about? Could be the yummy fruit, fish and cheese at the Kensington markets.

below **Papineauville, Québec** The Beast's *doppelgänger*, trophied like a trout on a wall.

opposite left Québec City, Québec A crowd waits for street theatre in one of Place Royale's cobbled corners.

opposite right Ottawa, Ontario Sareb (in scarlet tunic) and Linus do their duty on Parliament Hill.

opposite below Grande-Anse, New Brunswick Acadian patriotism paints a house red, white and blue.

right near Cap-Pelé, New Brunswick A tin rocket waits for lift-off at Desiré Goguen's outdoor folk-art museum.

below Shediac, New Brunswick This giant lobster is more than a mouthful.

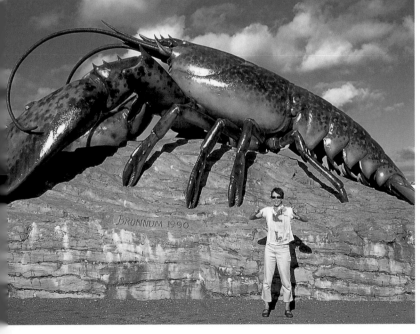

left Prince Edward Island's red-sand beaches tempt the tootsies.

below Abram-Village, Prince Edward Island Les Singes – monkeys – are a barrel of laughs at an Acadian festival.

opposite Lunenburg, Nova Scotia The Beast goes dockside at a rum-runner's haven.

opposite below left East River, Nova Scotia Fred Cook's hub-cap collection has none for old Chevys.

opposite below right Windsor, Nova Scotia Giant pumpkin king Howard Dill with one of his paunchy veggies.

opposite Hall's Harbour, Nova Scotia The tide's way, way out at the Bay of Fundy.

above Twillingate, Newfoundland Melvin Horwood's wharf museum remembers the cod.

right / below Rose Blanche, Newfoundland This little outport is the prettiest of them all.

above Dildo, Newfoundland
What's in a name? No-one
knows, but the locals like it.

right Bonavista Peninsula,
Newfoundland A zany
lighthouse rewards a walk on
the wild and windy side.

The market was not what I'd expected. I naively imagined rows of fresh loaves, squishy cheese, crunchy veggies – all the goods you'd find in a little French provincial town. Instead, crowds haggled for sombreros and fringed lampshades, dalmatian-dog patterned blankets and a trophy plaque of miniature hockey pucks from all the teams across Canada.

After a solid hour of roaming up and down lines of polyester pants and gap-toothed handsaws I found the fresh bread, cheese and veggies tucked away at the back. These were a bargain but came with a catch: you had to buy three pots of peppers or half a gross of potatoes or a gorilla's-breakfast-sized bunch of bananas. So I did. As expected the fruit and veggies rotted in the car. It stank like a compost heap for a week.

In Québec, as in other parts of the country, road crews doing *travaux* blocked the highway willy nilly. *Travaux* became a catch phrase. Not another *travaux*, we groaned, at the sight of signalmen holding the *Arrêt* sign. *Travaux* really translated as 'chaos'. The signalmen at either end apparently had had a tiff and weren't speaking, or had wandered off for lunch without telling their counterpart. Cars drove higgledy piggledy both ways on the one-way strip. Nobody waited their turn. In the imbroglio the Beast nicely managed a little cross-country sojourn through a potato field.

Niagara Falls, Toronto and Ottawa had citied us out for a little while. Not that we hadn't enjoyed them – we had, hugely – but even Montréal's élan and fabulous cuisine didn't tempt us. I expected to find fabulous cuisine everywhere. Plus, I was holding out for my favourite city in Canada, Québec City. On the map all roads led to Montréal except a thin black line snaking along to Trois-Rivières and then to Québec City. We seized it gladly.

At St-Jacques I looked for a picnic stop to munch the Lachute loaves and cheese. But a drizzly rain had started to fall, so we pulled into a roadside café. In my best French I ordered chicken and rice soup for Ken and fish and chips *pour moi*. Ken's soup soon appeared. He pronounced it hot and adequate in the chicken and rice department. I waited for my fish and chips. And waited. And waited some more. Then decided to end the waiting by visiting the loo, which inevitably prompted meal delivery the minute I left the table.

On my return the fish and chips struck me dumb in two languages. I didn't recall ordering Fish Doing Dead Man's Float in Greasy Puddle and Corpse-Finger Fries but perhaps, my French being what it was, I had. I ate the crackers from Ken's soup and called it lunch. It was obviously *très stupide* to order something as English as fish and chips in a Québec diner.

At the counter the waitress asked a question in French. She tried again, and finally asked in English, 'Was it good?'

Oh dear.

'Non.' I shook my head mournfully.

'Non?' She looked aghast. 'Un moment, wait here please.' She disappeared off towards the kitchen. In *un moment* she returned.

'You pay only for the soup.'

So I did.

Trois-Rivières is the second-oldest city in North America, after Québec City. Of the many attractions – latte *avec croissant* at a quaint café, a heritage walk – we chose a cautionary tour of the old prison, where all the tour guides were ex-inmates.

Our guide, Raymond, had marked off three long, soul-searing months 'inside' on drug charges in the early seventies. 'I was into peace and love,' he said, moody as a mud hen, 'and they put me in with robbers. It was a school of crime.'

This dank pile of stone was Canada's oldest jail. It was now a historic monument. Raymond hated it so fiercely he nearly lifted off the cement floor as he showed our group around.

'Do you 'ear that sound, the sound of the door closing? It makes me ill at my stomach to 'ear it.'

We followed Raymond up and down and along the narrow grey corridors. It wasn't a place you'd want to spend much time, but I'd visited gloomy Alcatraz in San Francisco. This didn't look any worse.

Apparently, it was. 'You see 'ere, this cell, it is for two prisoners, we were nine. We 'ad a shower once a week, a shit bucket for a toilet.'

Raymond had passed the hours building the Eiffel Tower out of toothpicks with an old guy who'd been there forever.

The women's accommodation put me off any nascent thoughts of a life of crime. The long-gone inmates, mostly prostitutes warring for turf, threw the shit buckets at each other. The guards locked up each spatting cat separately in wire chicken cages the width of a steel bed for their own protection.

'It was a disgrace. A disgrace! We were humans, not animals. But we were treated like animals.'

Politicians vowed to do something about the prison but regularly failed to keep their promises. So the guards, who were sick and tired of working in a draughty, cold historic monument, alerted Amnesty International and the press. The fallout so embarrassed the government they shut the prison down in 1986.

I asked Raymond why, if he loathed the place so much, he kept coming back.

He smiled. 'I know I can leave.'

My delightful *belle soeur*, my brother's wife, is a Trois-Rivières native. She'd suggested taking the Chemin du Roy, the old King's Road, to Québec City along Highway 138 instead of the multilane Highway 40. We'd missed the part running from Montréal to Trois-Rivières, but the villages scattered along the next bit of Canada's oldest carriageway were as charming as a sweet old *grand-mère* in a frilly cloth bonnet. In Deschambault lace curtains twitched on yellow-and-blue verandahed houses as the Beast rumbled through. In Cap-Santé and Neuville the Chemin du Roy meandered past neat whitewashed stone houses set along cobbled lanes older than Canada itself.

The road pottered along the banks of the St Lawrence River, where ships bound for the rest of the world steamed along the same St Lawrence seaway French explorer Jacques Cartier sailed down in the 1530s. Cartier called the land he explored 'Kanata', from a Huron-Iroquois word meaning 'collection of huts'. The country's founding fathers mulled over many strange and wonderful names for the new land. If sage heads hadn't prevailed, the country's citizens would now be singing 'O Borealia' at the RCMP Musical Ride. Or watching *Hockey Night in Ursalia* on television. Or writing 'Victorialander' on immigration forms.

We dallied through bosky groves and over rolling hills until, with barely a moment's warning, the highway flung us into the old quarter of Québec City. Ken and I once stood, awed as church mice, outside the old city's most venerable hotel, the fairytale Château Frontenac. I vowed to stay there one day. Today was the day.

I'd grown weary of grubbing around at groundhog level amongst the kindling and ankle-biting insects. While flicking through some brochures in a damp Trois-Rivières campground I'd spotted an ad for the Château promising such potent restoratives as a spa pool, room service and a bed free from the smell of rotten spuds. I reached for the Cellphone That Never Rang and made a call.

Old Québec City is still the walled fortress it was before 1759 when the French general Montcalm lost a battle on the Plains of Abraham outside the city to his English counterpart Wolfe, setting up the French to lose the entire war and their New France goodies a handful of years later. Forced to choose between colonies, France kept hold of warm Guadeloupe instead of cold Canada, in a decision so ill-considered it must have been a coin toss (Heads! Guadeloupe! Grab the beach towels!).

If only Montcalm had held the line would the rest of Canada be like this I wondered, as I giggled at the Place Royale street theatre, watched a single nun in simple blue glide through the doors of the Notre Dame cathedral, listened to the cloppity clop of horse hooves on cobbles, sipped *soupe à l'oignon gratinée* while perched on vinyl stools at the counter at Le Buffet de l'Antiquaire on rue St-Paul (the gas flame under the blackened pots so close it beaded sweat on the diner's brow), peered through lace curtains patterned with women gathering wheat at the window of appartement 27^1/2 rue St-Somebody and smelled the windowbox geraniums, red against periwinkle shutters.

At sunset the tourist hordes, us among them, poured in invading English forces over the cobbles to dine, shop and watch the buskers wearing horse tails on unicycles, a classical guitarist flanked by six large white samoyeds, and a pair of gymnasts doing handstands. In a narrow lane near the Château the shops sold nothing but engravings and paintings and etchings and sketchings of the hotel.

'You like these?' asked François, resplendent in a black pork-pie hat and yellow trousers. He was an artists' agent, and an actor who'd been in a Mexican soap opera. *Vive le* free trade.

In Québec City, more than twenty-five years earlier, we'd eaten our first ever al fresco meal. I'd forgotten which restaurant it was, but Les Frères de la Côte made a fine stand-in. We dined on *escargots, gigot d'agneau, filet du saumon* and a whole lot of wine.

'I am 'appy you are speaking French,' said Karine the waitress. If reading French words off the menu counted as conversation, fine with me.

Karine must have put in a good word with the chef. The snails, lamb and salmon more than made up for the St-Jacques fish and chips experience. And so we strolled back along the cobbles to the fairytale hotel with the view of the Big Dipper from our rooftop window, to the spa pool and soft spud-free bed.

I didn't want to leave the Château. I could easily have lived there forever.

'They'll find you in there,' said Ken in the morning, prising me kicking and yowling out of the wardrobe.

Québec City didn't want us to leave, either. We twisted and turned and backed and forthed over many, many of the old quarter's narrow lanes before stumbling on the way out. The streets were built for horses, not our kind of Beast.

The Chemin du Roy ended at Québec City but the sweet wee villages carried on through the Charlevoix region. At Baie-St-Paul we snooped around rue St-Joseph, a historic street of pretty old homes with mansard roofs. A sign on one of the pretty old homes said 'Boulangerie Louise'. Hurrah. Fresh bread. Baguette for lunch. I opened the shop door and walked straight into somebody's mother's kitchen.

'Bienvenue!' shouted a cheerful doughy woman at the kitchen table. Louise, I presumed.

'I am making pizza to an old Italian recipe,' said Louise, enthusiastically chopping up a table-sized pizza.

'Are you Italian?'

'Non! I am many generations French Canadian.'

Piles of bread covered every table, bench and chair, even the washing machine and drier. There were fresh baguettes and wholesome loaves – apple and cinnamon, honey and walnut. Faced with so much choice I lost my nerve and bought a simple baguette. Boulangerie Louise solved a little mystery. I'd been looking in the wrong places for bakeries. In future all we had to do was find somebody's mother and follow her to her kitchen.

At St-Siméon a ferry crossed the St Lawrence to Rivière-du-Loup. The ferry workers packed the cars in tight as herrings, with barely a licence plate between them. But the hour-long crossing was, like the Lake Huron ride, perfectly flat, and the day fine and warm enough to stand outside in the breeze.

'Aw, fuck,' said the passenger next to me, peering through his binoculars.

I was a little taken aback. Maybe he'd seen something nobody else had, perhaps a hurricane or an unfriendly warship, or maybe somebody had dropped something essential overboard, like themselves.

But then a sleek black head popped out of the water. A seal. *Un phoque.*

Rivière-du-Loup (Wolf River) was disappointingly free of wolves. But one of the terror trucks lay on its side in the ditch. The driver had long since been hauled off, and a queue of traffic waited while rescuers worked to lift the truck from its resting place. Ken let out a low cheer and took a photo.

Most of the ferry traffic zapped off down the Trans-Canada Highway to New Brunswick and the shortest route into the maritime provinces. We'd already decided to spend a few days on the Gaspé Peninsula, then take the back way into New Brunswick. But first we had a date with a campground.

The Trois-Pistoles campground was the place where long ago we'd bought wine and got so excited about camping Québec-style. A grump of an old woman in the shop who spoke not a word of English had sold us a bottle. She had then sent us off to a solitary dirt patch on the river. We drank the wine. The sun set golden over the river. It was fabulous.

Trois-Pistoles wasn't hard to find – the colossal Notre-Dame-des-Neiges church in the town's centre dominated the landscape for miles around. The campground, though, proved more elusive.

'Do you remember this road?'

'Hmm. No. Not really. Not at all. Where are we?'

The road had had a facelift, as had everything else in the campground. The cramped old shop now had the antiseptic feel of a 7-Eleven. The old woman was gone, perhaps to her just reward. In her place a sullen snip of a girl sulked behind the counter. Not a single bottle of wine could be found anywhere on the new clean shelves. We stayed anyway, for old times' sake.

While waiting for the girl to choose a dirt patch to put us on I tried my best to answer questions about the Beast from a mustachioed gentleman from Montréal. This called for a quick brush-up on French words for numbers above fifty.

'C'est une cinquante-sept?'

'Non—'

'Cinquante-cinq?'

'Non, cinquante-six.'

'I am 'appy you are speaking French,' he said. 'There are people in Montréal who speak only English!'

Along the river the campers were packed in like herrings. The sun set golden over the river, but there was no wine to toast it with. Still, it was good to be back.

If the Beast had been feeling a little ignored through Manitoba and Ontario, the Québécois made up for it. At petrol stations, scenic spots or even just driving through a village, the townsfolk waved and shouted French numbers. Ken couldn't stop for a private contemplation of a mossy tree along a deserted stretch of road lest a classic-car fan pop up from behind a bush and catch him unzipped. At a fishing and hunting shop I somehow mistook for a small supermarket the proprietor laughed when I explained I was looking for milk. But he came out of the shop to look at the car.

'C'est magnifique! My brudder, 'e like dis car. 'E go to Cuba, 'e bring back a 'undred photo. I tink maybe of nice women but no. All of old car.'

The Beast was indeed magnificent. Ken washed the road dirt off the Beast's face, rump and underbelly whenever he got a chance. In rare idle moments he polished chrome or fiddled with engine bits, just because it was interesting, and he could.

'You know what I like about this car? There's nothing digital or electronic. No plastic, it's all metal. No air con, no power steering, just raw power.'

The new transmission didn't leak a drop. The car still started first time, every time, damp or dry weather. Sometimes I'd run my hand over the curve of a bumper or stroke the Chevy 'bird' on the bonnet. This car was so, so classy.

'Maybe we *should* keep the car,' Ken suggested more than once.

There might not be any choice. Only a few weeks remained of the trip, and still no buyers. Goodwill and lavish compliments were all very well but didn't put money in the pocket or solve the 'where to now' problem for the Beast. Throughout English Canada, whenever Ken mentioned the asking price people either backed away as if he'd offered them a dead gopher or nearly choked on their supersized Slurpees. A French-Canadian buyer seemed even less likely. We decided to forget about the whole business until after Québec. For the moment we'd bask in the Chevy's reflected glory.

The Beast rolled happily over the Gaspé Peninsula's coastal roads. Few tourists or trucks travelled this far-flung bit of Canada, so us idling along at forty or fifty miles per hour seeing the sights bothered nobody. The saints gathered steam up this coast. St

Mathieu, St Fabien, Ste Oldie, Ste Luce, Ste Flavie, Ste Félicité – the list was long. Most villages had their own immaculate church to tend to their couple of hundred souls. Gaspesians also took immense pride in their modest but neat-as-a-pin houses, some quirkily wider at the top than at the bottom, in Chinese takeout noodle box style. Flowers in painted pots cheered up every doorway. There was not a speck of graffiti anywhere.

There wasn't too much in the way of *boulangeries* or supermarkets either, although signs saying 'Homard 1 km' promised lobster lunch. At Sandwicherie des Capucins near Cap-Chat I could take it no more. We snacked on fresh lobster in a crisp panini with pungent garlic aioli and at ten dollars for the lot counted it a lucky find. The sandwicherie's unusual white sign reminded me of something.

'It's the blade from a wind turbine,' said Ken, who knew a blade from a wind turbine when he saw one. So it was. And somehow, not a surprise. Wind kept us constant company. Scarecrows standing in the fields barely kept their rags on. There was a *parc éolien*, a wind farm, nearby. We blew up the road for a look.

The Gaspé Peninsula was one of the windiest places in Canada. Wind farms on the peninsula supplied a third of the country's wind energy. The park was named for Aeolus, the Greek god of wind. All this and more our jolly guide Pierre told us while showing off the king of wind turbines – Éole, the world's tallest vertical-axis wind turbine. It resembled nothing so much as a giant two-bladed egg beater. Pierre shared all sorts of facts, figures and jokes. In case you never get to meet Pierre, here they are.

The bolts holding the thing together weighed 190 kilograms each. 'You need a big bowl of cereal and a banana to lift one of those – that is a good joke, ha ha!' laughed Pierre. The turbine needed 25 kilometres per hour of wind from any direction to push it, but couldn't take more than 63 kilometres per hour. It was 110 metres tall, 64 metres wide and weighed 400 tonnes. A helicopter could fly through it without touching the blades. Éole was built as an experiment. It hadn't turned in the wind for more than twenty years.

'Canadians are the most advanced in the world with this

technology. We don't only have a hockey team. That is a good joke!'

Farmers' fears about Éole's effects on dairy cows and migrating birds were unfounded, said Pierre. 'The cows do not give yoghurt. A study was done on the birds. One bird was killed. The study showed he forgot his glasses. Ha ha!' That was a good joke, we agreed.

At a small *marché aux puces* down the road a weather-rubbed ruffian hawked moose decoys from a trailer. The foam moose heads might fool a bird without its glasses from a hundred wing flaps away, but any self-respecting moose could tell this was not the mate of its dreams.

The moose decoy salesman wanted to move to New Zealand. 'Nouvelle-Zélande, c'est belle.'

I tried to explain that he might need another line of work, perhaps as a geologist or aircraft designer. The moose decoy business could be a little slow.

The eastern edge of the Gaspé Peninsula unspooled like a hand-coloured classic film; slowly, with gentle allure. La Martre lighthouse marked out a red wooden octagon on a grassy hill, its jewel of a glass prism brighter than a diamond. Rivers ran fat with salmon at Mont-Louis, where we stayed in a small *auberge* in a room papered with violets and overlooking the water and ate *tartes aux pommes avec* rum sauce by the light of a thumbnail moon. At Ste-Madeleine-de-la-Rivière-Madeleine another lighthouse stood in wood, this one a bridal white with a crimson roof. We bought cinnamon brioche at Grande-Vallée and licked crumbs off our fingers lying on sun-warmed chaises longues.

Pointe-à-la-Frégate. A line of model wooden ships sailing into the east along a rail. Their maker, a craftsman for forty years, yarned with a couple of mates in rocking chairs inside a dim shed with stacks of fragrant cedar and smooth polished boats. He laughed shyly and shook his head when asked to pose for a photo with his boats. He posed anyway. Near the village, an honour guard of seals flanked a pod of porpoises.

Cap-des-Rosiers. The scent of wild roses delicate on the summer wind. The highest lighthouse in the land stood sentry on stones like the ones that made it. And at last Percé. So beautiful, the road winding down to the village unbeatably dramatic; Percé Rock a levitating anvil in the hammered-steel sea. But in this most luminous of spots, so much traffic, so many tourist shops, so many tourists. Including us, of course.

The film clattered to a halt.

The campground at Pabos, once we found it down a back lane and over some railway tracks, was hard to miss. A plastic Santa beckoned campers at the gate.

'Qu'est-ce que le Santa is all about?' I asked the camp attendant.

'Noël Le Camping,' he replied mysteriously.

A summer Christmas in New Zealand still felt strange, but barbecues and beach picnics instead of turkey and trimmings had its advantages. A summer Christmas in Canada – that was just plain sacrilege. I hailed a couple of campers enjoying a quiet drink under their festive tinsel candy canes and illuminated jingle bells. The couple, Claude and Lorna, lived in Chandler, a ten-minute drive away. They spent every summer at the Pabos campground.

And why not? The campground rated near the top on my 'best campground yet' list. Each nicely wooded site had a neat Wedgwood-blue signpost hung with a basket of red geraniums. The picnic table and garbage box were painted a matching blue. Campers strolling among the plastic reindeer, snowmen and twinkling electric candles greeted each other like old friends. No doubt they were.

Claude spoke no English so Lorna solved the Noël mystery. Sort of. The campground's inhabitants decked their halls with boughs and tinsel every year to bid farewell to summer. Next weekend there'd be a pétanque tournament, dances, horseshoes, a corn roast, gifts for the kiddies, even a Santa parade. Next weekend.

We'd be in Nova Scotia by then. Bah, humbug.

I had one more question, not a Christmassy one. The Québec flag flapped on flagpoles all over the Gaspé Peninsula but I'd not seen a single Canadian maple leaf. My French, I felt, had improved enough to discuss politics.

'Est-ce que vous feel more Québécois ou Canadian?'

Lorna translated Claude's reply. 'Lately, more like Québécois. There's so much government scandal. The government does nothing for the people of the area.'

East or west, French or English, the people felt the same. Crooks ran the country. They ate cake while the people scrounged for stale breadcrumbs. A rebellion could be a-brewing. Probably not in this lifetime, but maybe the next, visitors might show their passports at the border of the République Révolutionnaire du Québec or the Defiant Democracy of Alberta.

A crowd of shirtless beer-drinking men and elegant wine-sipping women sauntering down the road skirmished into our campsite when they spied the Beast.

'C'est magnifique!'

'C'est superbe!'

'Seats a whole baseball team – but not a whole football team,' quipped a hairy fellow reading the for sale ad. 'Ha ha! Parlez-vous français? Do you speak French?'

'Un peu seulement.'

'A leetle, eh. Enough to save your life! Ha ha! I am 'appy you are speaking French. We can look?'

They flung open the doors and crawled inside. Honked the horn. Made V8 vroom vroom noises and pretended to drive. We all toasted the Beast, *la voiture magnifique*. The elegant women and shirtless men bustled off in merry mayhem.

The slogan on the Québec licence plate is 'Je me souviens'. I remember. Remember what, exactly, nobody seemed to know. Some said it meant remember Montcalm's thrashing on the Plains of Abraham, and weep. Maybe it just meant remember Québec.

Hard not to, really.

The Acadian Way

'The best thing to set indigo dye in clothes
is the urine of pure adolescent boys.'

*Villager, Historic Acadian Village,
near Caraquet, New Brunswick*

Crossing the Patapédia River into New Brunswick did not mean a return to the land of total English immersion. Far from it. At Campbellton a left turn led to the French-speaking Acadian Peninsula, a right turn to the province's more Anglicised interior. We lingered in Campbellton only long enough to view a giant leaping salmon. Then took a left.

At first the route didn't impress: near the industrial town of Dalhousie, factory stacks poured thick grey smoke into the sky. But soon the noxious factories petered out and small fishing towns petered in, although so far it wasn't very French. A fisherman shaking out mackerel nets on a Charlo beach spoke in a broad Scots brogue, as did the Loonieland sales assistant at Jacquet River, where I traded a loonie for a paring knife to add to the cutlery collection.

'What's that for?' said Ken.

'We're missing a knife. I must have left it at one of the campgrounds.'

'When was the last time you saw it?'

'Ontario somewhere, I think.'

Ken whistled a few bars of 'Killer on the Road'.

We amused ourselves playing spot the best lawn ornament. Most gardens sprouted at least one. Many people had apparently called in at a lawn ornament auction and, unable to stop themselves, bought the lot. Ken spotted a life-sized stag, a small boy in breeches, a family of plywood bears. I spied kissing couples, wheelbarrows, cats, dogs, ducks. Miniature lighthouses topped the 'most popular' list. Then we both spotted bonneted girls in dresses painted red, white and blue with a yellow star. We were closing in on the Acadians.

Acadians lived in Canada long before it was Canada. These

farming folk took hoe and plough and left France at the turn of the seventeenth century for the French colony of Acadie, in what is now New Brunswick, Nova Scotia and Prince Edward Island. The Acadian flag copied the French tricolour; the gold star, the Stella Maris, stood in for the Virgin Mary, the Acadian patron saint.

For another 150 years things went as well as could be expected for peasant pawns farming land France and England fought like cats and dogs to plunder. History recorded what happened. The French lost. *Je me souviens.* The English kicked out Acadians in their thousands during *le grand dérangement*, the great expulsion. They fled hither and thither, some as far as Louisiana, where the people called them Cajuns. Some Acadians were allowed to return a decade later, but only to fish, not to farm.

The previous year had been the Acadians' 400th anniversary celebrations. Acadians splashed out so enthusiastically there wouldn't have been a pot of red, white or blue paint left in the land. At Pointe-Verte all the telephone poles sported Acadian colours to their waists. Acadian flags flew from mailboxes, decks, dump trucks, church spires and some energetic souls near Grande-Anse had done up their entire house in flag-like fashion.

Bedazzled by this patriotic panorama Ken didn't even complain when I casually directed him to the Village Historique Acadien a short way down the road.

'What is this?' he asked, suspicious of ending up in some boring historical reconstruction of life in Acadia.

'It's a farm. You'll like it,' I said, paying for two tickets to the historical reconstruction of life in Acadia.

'It'd better not be boring. If it's boring I'm going for a nap in the Chevy.'

It could have been boring. It wasn't, not a bit. Who knew that the best thing to set indigo dye in clothes was the urine of 'pure' adolescent boys? We spent a lazy afternoon ambling along shady lanes, watching women in bonnets and home-made clothes bake bread, spin yarn or weave linen from flax. Men in baggy breeches and braided-oat hats carved wooden clogs or forged nails. Happy barnyard animals nudged up for a pat. These useful practical skills were just the things we were going to need when the planet's electrical grid fizzled out.

The original houses and barns dated from the late 1700s to the mid 1930s. All had been ferreted out from farms and villages, dismantled brick by brick, board by board, and put back together in the ultimate challenge of 'insert tab A into slot B'. Even Ken was pleased he'd come. I left well satisfied, except for one thing; I was on the hunt for an Acadian festival, one with fiddlers fiddling and ancient games of chance.

'No,' said one of the spinning ladies, who as well as speaking fluent French spoke perfect English. 'Nothing around here. The summer's almost gone. Try asking at Caraquet. Nearly everyone there is Acadian.'

There were no festivals at Caraquet. The town did, though, offer such amenities as laundromats and fast-food outlets, so for an oblivious hour I watched clothes go round and round. Ken talked cars with the laundromat owner.

'C'est une cinquante-six?'

'Oui,' said Ken nonchalantly.

The laundromat man owned a 1968 Thunderbird. He showed Ken a photo. He spoke no English. Ken spoke little French. The car lovers conversed at length in the universal language of pointing at things under the bonnet.

Across the country we'd avoided fast-food joints, those rapacious modern-day empire builders. But by the time I'd folded the last T-shirt, A&W burgers were the only things available for dinner.

I didn't mind too much – I'd always had a soft spot for A&W. Like drive-in movies, cruisin' the Dub was a teenage weekend pastime of bygone years; the first A&W drive-in burger joint in Canada appeared in the same year as our Chevy. It was an idea born of the cult of the car. You parked your car with all the other classics and shouted your order into a speaker only marginally less tinny than the ones at the drive-in movies. The car-hop girls loaded trays of root beer, onion rings and Teenburgers onto the car's rolled-down window. You sat next to your honey on the bench seat of a '63 Pontiac slurping root beer, looking at all the other couples slurping root beer in their '59 Fords or '56 Dodges looking at you looking at them. The boys just looked at the cars.

The car-hop girls had gone the way of *T. rex*, but the food hadn't changed. As we sat outside munching Teenburgers a couple going into the restaurant detoured to our table.

'C'est une—'

'Cinquante-six,' said Ken, who was fast becoming fluent.

'Ah, a '56! Like the one I courted my wife in. It worked, you see?'

The lady in question blushed.

'I kept the woman but lost the car somehow.'

The kept woman sped inside to order burgers.

'Let me tell you a secret,' confided the man. 'I am looking for a 1956 two-tone green sedan, like the one I had when I met my wife. I want to buy it as a surprise for our fiftieth wedding anniversary. A good surprise, no? But they are hard to find.'

Yes. So why not buy a sensational '56 two-tone copper and cream station wagon? Like the one right here.

'Ah, c'est belle. But it must be a two-tone green sedan.'

The car-selling situation was becoming serious. If even a dedicated Chevy fan with money to burn wasn't interested in our poor Beast, who was? There wasn't much time left before the end of September and literally the end of the road. Ken steeled himself for the taste of humble pie and called Saskatoon Chevy Fan. Saskatoon Chevy Fan hemmed and hawed and said he really wanted a '57 Chevy. He'd think about it.

Ken called Bruce. 'What do you think? Any ideas?' Bruce generously refrained from pointing out the obvious: we should have taken the guy's money when he waggled it at us and ran.

'There's always the Internet,' he said.

Fergawdsake. That had as much appeal as a sharp stick in the eye. The Internet Beast-buying experience still lingered like a bad smell; I wanted nothing more to do with the whole online etherworld. Ken ticked off our options. Sell the car online. Or... hmmm. Sell the car online.

The campground owner at Caraquet loved old cars. So much so that the whole campground was soon going to be full of classic cars at a Show 'n' Shine event. There'd be oodles of car lovers and possible car buyers. How soon was this? Next weekend. Naturally. We'd be nowhere near the place.

So online auction it was. The sympathetic campground owner kindly offered the use of his office phone line to do the deed. Ken parked the car in a scenic but slightly sloping grassy spot on the edge of a high bank overlooking the sea. We walked back to the office, expecting to have the whole business finished in no time. Two hours and much cursing later the online ad was live. It hadn't been easy. Either we were just not net savvy or the website really was an evil labyrinth dreamt up by sadists who camped in Manitoba on weekends.

While we'd been wrestling with the Internet a heavy rain had burst from the clouds. We splashed in total blackness through ankle-deep puddles, wriggled sodden into the car and called it a night. During the night I had an unsettling dream. In this dream the Beast slid slowly backwards over the slippery grass, down the grassy bank and into the sea, hindquarters crumpled, snout pointing skywards. I woke up, sweating. Ken had woken up too. He'd been listening to the pouring rain, and thinking.

I told him my dream. 'At least we're not moving,' I said.

There was a pause. Then Ken said, 'How do you know?'

We sprang into spine-tingling action. Ken leapt stark naked into the black rainy night. He heaved the food crates into the back. I manhandled the crates into position, urging him on. He slid onto the driver's seat. Groped for the headlight switch. Pulled the knob clean off the windshield wiper switch. Feck! Found the headlight switch. Turned on the lights. Started the car. Which somehow was in reverse. The Beast lurched backwards towards the sea. Feck! Clinging to the bench seat, the sarong curtain flapping round my ears, I squawked like a strangled chook. Feck! Ken dropped the transmission into drive. Slowly, slowly, he inched the car over the wet grass, taking care not to run over any tents disguised as lumps of black night. We reparked the Beast on a level site many metres away from the high bank and the greedy sea.

The rain fell all through the next day. It was going to be a long one. Another generous friend had issued an invitation, nay, an edict, to visit her at her Prince Edward Island (PEI) cottage. Our friend was a hostess extraordinaire, so we were only too pleased to accept. After the previous night's leaping about in the rain, this sounded wonderful. But a fair chunk of New Brunswick still stood between us and PEI.

Not that I didn't like New Brunswick. I did, very much. We'd almost lived there once. Fresh from pharmacy college I'd been offered a job in Chatham, just down the coast from Caraquet. But on a reconnaissance visit, tiny Chatham made Saskatoon seem like New York City. It was the sort of place where Mom's second rule of travel applied: Say hello to everyone you meet or they'll think you're stuck up. Everybody knew everybody else. As the town's only pharmacist I'd end up knowing everything about everybody and dodging people also wanting to know everything about everybody. That may have been wholly unfair, but I didn't take the job.

If I couldn't find a festival, then real Acadian food would have to do. At Neguac I spotted a small café, named something along the lines of Authentic Acadian Café, off the main road. Ken ordered a meat and veggie pie. I ordered *poutine rapée*. I wasn't sure what the *rapée* part meant, but one could never have too much poutine.

The waitress explained the Acadian-Cajun situation. 'Cajuns are our cousins,' she said. 'There is a unity between us. They come to our celebrations and we go to theirs.'

Foodwise, the Acadians might get the better end of that exchange. Ken dug territorially into his tender meat and veggie pie. I stared down at a gelatinous blind eye of Cyclops wondering how, once again, I'd got it so wrong. The waitress explained what the strange baseball-sized thing was: a ball of grated (that was the *rapée* part) raw and mashed potato, stuffed with seasoned pork, boiled for three hours and served in the meat's juices.

'But why is it called poutine?' I whined.

She shrugged. 'I don't know. It just is.'

I attacked the slithery orb with every bit of available cutlery. It cannonballed off the plate in an attempt to escape across the floor. I retrieved it from the tablecloth, snuck up on it from above and skewered it.

Looks deceived. It tasted of pork and mashed potato and pork juice, quite nice. In fact, very nice. I ate the whole thing. An hour later the vengeful *poutine rapée* regrouped and swelled into a basketball-sized lump. I lay in the back of the car, slowly deflating.

Near Cap-Luminère a brace of festively painted fishing buoys brightened a fence. These were exactly the sort of souvenir I wanted to bring back: something seafaring, decorative and far too ungainly to fit in a suitcase.

Ken shook his head. 'Uh uh. Buy a fridge magnet.'

At a small souvenir shop the shopgirl looked hopeful as I browsed the mussel-shell wreaths and dried starfish painted in Acadian colours.

'How's business?' I asked.

'Things aren't so good here. There aren't so many lobsters now. Some people work in shops but in winter most fishermen are on food stamps. But hey, what doesn't kill you...'

I bought a painted starfish.

Near Bouctouche the drizzle hardened to a pelting rain. The Chevy's windshield wipers gathered enough strength to beat a steady rhythm.

'Bouc touche bouc touche bouc touche,' I blathered, for want of anything else to say.

'Your brain's getting low on oxygen,' said Ken.

We ate an oxygen-replenishing lobster roll at a roadside fish stand. It was divine, as only a fresh crustacean in a bread roll can be. We tipped the waitress.

She tipped us in return. 'The price of gas is going to a dollar thirty – cars're lining up down the street for a fill.'

Ouch. That was going to hurt. Petrol cost a $1.08 per litre at the last fill-up. Hurricane Katrina, in that careless way of natural disasters, had just beaten New Orleans to a watery mess and, as an afterthought, bumped off some oil rigs. Acadians and Cajuns shared more than food and festivities. This rain was Katrina's tail.

Outside Shediac the pelting rain upgraded to an obliterating downpour. The wipers struggled to cope. There was no such thing as 'automatic' with these cable-operated wipers, so Ken kept an eye on the fast-disappearing road while hand-tweaking them. They grumped and thumped, grumped and thumped.

'That doesn't sound right,' I said.

The wipers grumped, flung themselves to the outer edges of the windshield, thumped, and died.

'I can't see a thing.'

Ken wound down his window. A gush of rain drenched him in seconds.

We pulled over near the tourist information centre. Driving through a hurricane's tail at the mercy of melodramatic windshield wipers was a hazard to us and everybody in our path. Camping in it appealed even less than driving in it, so I slopped out of the car to ask about places to stay. I also inquired about a large boat, a small ship really, grounded just offshore in the harbour. Another of Katrina's victims?

'No. But it's stuck,' said the young woman pertly.

'Since when?'

'Three years.'

'Why is it still there?'

'We don't talk about that boat,' she retorted, her mouth a prim moue.

If I ever again found myself in New Brunswick needing a dry patch in a hurricane's tail I would head immediately to Shediac and stay there. No, why wait for a hurricane? Just go. Shediac lured with streets of heritage homes converted into sumptuous B&Bs supplying both B and B, plus more cheap fresh lobster than you could shake a painted starfish at. Our B&B, the Maison Tait, once accommodated a potato merchant. The rambling house sprawled around a welter of bedrooms capacious enough to do cartwheels in, as I found out to my pleasure. The potato business must have been a boomer.

The B&B owner knew the story of the beached boat in the harbour and he was happy to chat about it. The boat, a ferry on a test run, washed up on shore in a storm. The American owner washed his hands of it. The federal and provincial governments accused each other of responsibility. Stalemate.

'Some people worry it'll come loose and smash into the bridge. I kind of like the look of it. Gives the place character.'

Shediac needed no extra character. It was the lobster capital of the world. As proof, a giant roadside lobster, perfect in every lobsterish way, crawled up a rock across from the stranded ferry.

The rain dried up long enough for us to creep out to buy dinner supplies: a stick of garlic butter, some salad, strawberries, a bottle of Riesling, and two fat, freshly cooked lobsters, a breathtakingly cheap eight dollars a piece, at a lobster shed on the sea.

As a parting gift Katrina left behind a sultry evening. Ken parked the Chevy in a picnic spot overlooking the inner harbour, I laid the whole lobster feast out on the tailgate and we cracked open the lobster with a crescent wrench from the Beast's tool kit. This was a moose moment.

Albeit a little short-lived. A middle-aged couple, Edward and Doris, stopped to talk cars. This unending interest in the Chevy surprised me. I'd imagined a car as old and comely as the Beast might attract the odd hard-core classic-car enthusiast here and there, but almost always the people, usually men of baby boomer vintage, came up not to compare notes about a Beast of their own tucked away in a garage but to relive memorable times with a bygone four-wheeled love.

I had a '57 Chevy 150 Handyman/'71 Chevy truck/'69 Javelin/'67 Olds Dynamic 88/'59 Ford Crown Victoria/'56 Chevy Nomad. I drove to Alaska/California/Vancouver/spent all my money/lost my virginity in that car. I wish I still had it.

Our Beast reeled back the years. For these once-were-young-bucks, 'I wish I still had it' meant 'I wish I were still young, foolish and fancy-free enough to drive a '56 Chevy to California.' Of course, you could be middle-aged, foolish and temporarily fancy-free and still do this.

Edward's story went like this. His father died when he was thirteen. He wanted to buy a '53 Chevy but the bank wouldn't lend a skint sixteen-year-old the money. But his kind-hearted employer did – 'if you don't tell my sons'.

'Did ye ever hear of such a t'ing in yer time, sir? A deed like that, it stuck in the mind.'

Doris came from the area; that's why they moved back.

'We lived in Moncton, but they'll steal a toothpick if you leave it lying around.'

Add this to the list: Shediac was free of toothpick thieves.

The rain blew in again. We stayed another day at the B&B to practise cartwheels and check for potential buyers' emails on the laptop. Several auction watchers expressed interest. They wanted more photos. I sent them. They asked questions. Ken answered them. By the time we left Shediac, both of us felt sure some kind and loving Chevy fan would give our Beast a good home.

I didn't want to leave Maison Tait. Ken hauled me out kicking and yowling from under the bed.

'They'll find you under there, too.'

I wanted to make one more stop in New Brunswick, at the Musée d'art brut, an outdoor folk art museum at Cap-Pelé. Here broomstick women with tin can hats danced with old wringer washers, fishermen dogs rowed dinghies and Wallace and Gromit-style rockets waited for lift-off.

'Bonjour,' I called to a pair of old gents enjoying a smoke on the porch. 'Who makes these?'

'This old guy,' said one old gent, pointing to the other old gent. 'He's been making them for more than twenty years.'

'Eh? Qu'est-ce qu'elle dit?' said the other old gent. What's she saying? Desiré Goguen was a wee bit hard of hearing and I was a wee bit hard of French, so his porch buddy translated. 'He says he builds them to make people smile. Please, come and see. You are free to look.' And so I looked, and smiled. There were worse ways to while away retirement than crafting bits of old tin and lobster claws into whimsy to make people smile.

The Confederation Bridge linking New Brunswick to Prince Edward Island across the Northumberland Strait took ten minutes to cross whizzing along at a crisp eighty kilometres per hour. Nearly thirteen kilometres from one end to the other, it was the longest bridge over ice-covered water in the world. So said the

PEI tourist brochure, obviously clutching at a Guinness record.

The drive across PEI to our friend's cottage at Little Pond took quite a bit longer. PEI looked no bigger than a sprat on the map, but size deceived. Roads turned right and left and bent here, there and everywhere, with barely a straight line in sight. After a week of coastal driving, this trickery came as a shock to the navigator, who'd only had to keep the sea on the left ('this left, not the other left') to stay on track. A handful of U-turns later, enough order prevailed for both driver and navigator to enjoy the scenes of contented cows ruminating on farmlets set on sunny hillsides. The smell of the sea blew in one nostril, the scent of mown lawns in the other, all the way to Little Pond.

One of the nicest things about driving across the country of our birth, I'd come to realise, was the friends and relatives, some not seen for many years, some never seen before, who fêted and fed us so well our clothes shrunk at an alarming rate.

A life on a road unknown had a seductive siren call. What was down that road – a flat coyote? A moose moment? There was always something, even if at the time it seemed like not much. Not knowing who we'd meet, and where, and what would happen next, kept the wheels turning. But so too did indolent days shucking oysters by the sea with a cottageful of friends, walking and talking on red sand beaches, scattering sandpipers whistling like wind-up toys on the incoming tide, watching *Coronation Street* on Sundays, yakking about old times. And, all importantly, here was easy Internet access. The online bidding had already started, but the cheapskate bids didn't come close to the reserve price. But that was part of the thrill. Bruce, who'd been keeping an eagle eye on the auction, emailed encouragement. 'It's not over till it's over, kids.' Two days to showdown. We decided to stay on PEI until then.

'Did you know there's a New Zealand near here?' asked one of our cottage-mates over breakfast.

Here was another odd thing. We'd come in search of Canada but kept tripping over unexpected New Zealand connections. Perhaps this cross-planet pollination wasn't surprising. After all, we'd cross-pollinated the planet ourselves and fitted in with only minor bouts of culture shock. But finding an actual New Zealand in Canada took the proverbial cake.

Armed with an expanded map showing PEI to be the size of a walrus we set off to track it down. A sign on Highway 306 pointed to New Zealand straight ahead. Ken drove straight ahead. Nothing. Had the navigator messed up again? We turned around. Nothing. Then Ken spotted another sign nearly hidden, proclaiming a brambly patch to be New Zealand. The rest of New Zealand appeared to be three well-worn houses lacking so much as a hall or church or shop to stick them together. The sign needed an addition: 'New Zealand wuz here.'

Tourism PEI explained. The name New Zealand was given in jest in 1858, when settlers were immigrating to this small PEI town at the same time as others departed for the bigger New Zealand. I found out something else. There was an Acadian festival in Abram-Village and tomorrow was the last day.

I love festivals, any kind, big or small. The parades, the food, the music, crowds of happy people. This one promised all of that and something even more intriguing: cow bingo. Cows playing bingo? Bingo played on the hides of cows? I had to find out.

Ken would rather eat raw insects than fritter away a day on crowds, parades and log-rolling competitions but this parade lured him with the promise of classic cars. So once again we drove across the whole of PEI. It was well worth the trip. The crowd's biggest applause went to Les Singes Acadiens – young boys dressed up like monkeys in rain barrels attached to a revolving gizmo whirling them around in the air on the back of a truck. They threw bananas at the crowd. Their aim impressed me. The gizmo impressed Ken. The classic cars impressed us both.

This was the stuff of childhood memories. Over the years my parents had taken us to many Children's Day or Travellers' Day parades. Summer was not summer without a parade. This one had a similar nostalgic feel. The Acadian monkey boys replaced the Saskatoon Shriners – grown men in purple fezzes riding tiny motorcycles. Saskatoon parades had even more tractors, and usually some pretty horses. But, like folk art museums, they made me smile.

I went off to place some cow bingo bets.

'So you're gonna take a chance on the poop?' grinned the young ticket seller.

Everyone in the cottage at Little Pond wanted to bet a loonie on cow bingo. I chose five numbered squares from more than two thousand marked on a whiteboard. So did about two thousand other folk. Odds weren't looking good, but if we did win the prize we stood to gain half the cow bingo earnings, enough to buy petrol and lobster for the rest of the trip.

Cow bingo was the festival's grande finale, after the pig scramble. Hopeful cow bingoers abandoned the fiddlers and miniature horse shows to pack the grandstand. Three cows tottered out of a truck into a paddock marked off with string.

'Once there was one cow only for cow bingo. Now we have more than one, to make it faster,' explained the MC, which didn't really explain much at all.

The cows swished their tails. They gazed at whatever cows gazed at when a grandstand full of gambling folk was watching them. They nibbled straw left over from the pig scramble. A minute later a cow lifted its tail and splatted out a fat pat. One of the judges hurried out, stuck a straw in the middle of the pat, and measured its position. Then they matched the pat's whereabouts to the squares on the whiteboard. And it was all over for cow bingo. The MC announced the lucky winner. It wasn't us.

The online Chevy auction ended that night. We all crowded round the laptop, pulses racing. Serious Chevy Buyer, the person who'd asked the questions and done the homework, bid steadily. Only seconds stood between them and owning the Beast. We thought they'd won. They thought they'd won. Then with three seconds to go a complete unknown slapped on an extra few hundred bucks. The Beast had a new home, in Okotoks, Alberta.

We alerted Bruce, who was, after all, the legal owner, to be on the lookout for money coming his way.

'I've always wanted to go to Cuba,' said Bruce.

Coastal Classics

' The bigger the punkin, the happier folks are. '

Howard Dill, the giant pumpkin king,
Windsor, Nova Scotia

On the PEI–Nova Scotia ferry there was time for quiet contemplation.

'I'm going to miss that car,' said Ken.

I would, too. I liked cars, but usually not enough to miss them. The only other vehicle I'd ever truly fallen for, apart from the fantasy Cadillac, was a burnt-orange 1970 MGB convertible that taught me automobile love is rewarded by, yes, one heck of a good time, but also near death by drowning in thunderstorms and repair bills heftier than the car itself.

Still, we missed the Beast already, and it wasn't even gone yet. All the more reason to carry on cruising until the deal was done.

First up, a visit to some more large orange things: the giant pumpkins of Nova Scotia's Annapolis Valley. These podgy princes of the vegetable world appealed in a way no other vegetable did, not that I invested much time in dreaming about legumes. Giant Fake Things were good, Giant Real Things even better.

We'd just missed the town of Stanley's Sixteenth Annual Pumpkin Weigh-Off but a pair of giant pumpkins slumped abandoned outside the town hall. At a measly 379 and 421 pounds, according to the weights grease-pencilled on them, these lonely losers didn't have the stuff of which prize pumpkins are made. I gave them a hug anyway. My arms didn't even reach halfway around their bloated bellies.

We filled up at a wonderful old-style garage in Stanley, the kind where a grey-haired fellow in dusty coveralls who knows exactly where to find the petrol cap wanders out to fill up the car at a pump as old as himself. The kind with home baking for sale. While Ken dithered over the butter tarts and peanut-butter cookies I inquired about the whereabouts of other pumpkins.

'Go see Howie Dill's farm in Windsor. Over the bridge, turn

right, no left, no – you better ask when you get there. You can't miss it.'

'You can't miss it', I'd discovered from bitter experience, usually meant, 'You are doomed to drive around forever in some directionless vortex never coming close to the object of your desire.' But Howie Dill's farm truly was unmissable: a pumpkin festival all of its own. The giant pumpkins in Howie's patch had so long ago lost the svelte round shape of lesser pumpkins they sagged under their own pumpkin obesity into half-deflated beanbag shapes. But these were delicate vegetables: pumpkin houses kept the sun from scalding sensitive pumpkin skins.

Lean, blue-eyed Howie, breeder of the Atlantic Giant, was the undisputed giant pumpkin king of the world, although he was too modest to say so. He was a star member of the Giant Pumpkin Federation Hall of Fame.

Howie's family had lived on the farm for five generations. His father grew pumpkins. 'I've always been interested in punkins. I set out to improve on Dad's punkins. I didn't have a college education, no background in genetics. I selected the right plants, and things started to mushroom.'

Did they ever. Prize-winning pumpkins packed on 7 to 15 kilograms a day during their four-month gestation. I could almost see them growing.

Twenty-five years ago, said Howie, the first prize pumpkins topped the scales at almost 500 pounds – around 225 kilograms. Today those pulpy-fleshed runts wouldn't be plump enough to pull a major prize – Howie's top pumpkin weighed in at 980 pounds.

'The bigger the punkin, the happier folks are. They make people smile.'

How did he move these monsters?

'Get six or seven good men. Cut the punkin from its vine, then you slide a tarp under, and everybody lifts. You need a forklift to put the bigger ones on the scales.'

During the first Gulf War the US government bought one of Howie's giant pumpkins to cheer up dispirited pumpkinless American soldiers. Under a veil of secrecy the army loaded the paunchy veggie onto a plane and flew it to the Gulf under cover of darkness.

Howie liked that. 'The newspaper headline read, "Secret Weapon for Gulf War". Everybody thought it was some missile. It was just a giant punkin.'

The world record was 1469 pounds, a massive 666 kilograms. Cinderella could fit herself, her prince and the whole ugly step-family in that one. Or, like the keenest pumpkin lovers, she could float in it.

The Windsor Pumpkin Regatta on nearby Lake Pizaquid (first prize $1000 plus a large plaque) was next on the pumpkin events calendar. In what was becoming an annoyingly boring theme, we would be far away. This was such a popular event that US cable television channels came up to cover it. The first year attracted only five entrants but last year thirty-seven pumpkin paddlers and sailors took to the waves. Howie's son Danny had some top tips: 'Get a four-hundred- to five-hundred-pound pumpkin, hollow it out. You've got to get out quick before the wake hits you or you just bob all over.'

The rules of engagement were clear:

- The pumpkin must be in the water and contestants inside the pumpkin.
- No flotation devices allowed on exterior of pumpkin.
- The pumpkin can only be propelled by the person(s) in the pumpkin.
- There are two classes of competition: a) kayak, paddling, rowing and b) motors, sails. Competitors are encouraged to name and decorate their pumpkin.
- On completion of the race, entries will be inspected and certified by Ground Search and Rescue.

Presumably this last was to ensure all pumpkins were not plastic blow-ups in giant pumpkin disguise or unfloatworthy duds fitted with secret inflatable bladders.

Howie's love of pumpkins only slightly outweighed his interest in ice hockey. The first-ever ice hockey game in Canada was played in the 1800s on Long Pond on the Dills' family farm. The Dills, of course, were not responsible for the subsequent carnage on frozen ponds and rinks across the nation.

The world famous giant Bay of Fundy tides surged in and out only a leisurely half hour's drive away from Windsor. At the coastal hamlet of Hall's Harbour the tide had gone way out, to wherever tides go when they're not at the beach. Warpline-makers were doing brisk business on the Bay of Fundy. Fishing and sailing boats left as stranded as minnows on the outgoing tide idled twelve metres down from the wharf on the mud, waiting for the tide to come back from vacation. Boat owners miscalculating that height, say confusing feet with metres, could find their boat dangling like bait at the end of a too-short rope.

From high on the wharf I had a bird's eye view of fishermen on board the boats baiting their long lines for dogfish. Dogfish was a fall from grace. Giant salmon once littered the beach – no more. Lobster was once so common poor folks ate it at every meal – no more. In those bygone times of lobster excess, only special guests dined on that sought-after delicacy, bologna. Like most prairie children of the sixties I'd eaten plenty of bologna – fried or raw, with or without onions and ketchup. If only I'd known about the Nova Scotia lobster surplus, I'd have happily swapped some for a crate of bologna to help out the Nova Scotia poor folks.

A dolorous chap in the general store offered a taste of another local specialty, dulse. A pretty name for dried seaweed.

'It's good for you.' He pointed to a list of all the nutritious goodies in dulse, and cocked a hopeful eyebrow. Of course it was good for you. Anything tasting like a fermented compost heap or a fish's bladder always was. I hated to disappoint him, especially after he muttered, 'Lots of people come through here, but that doesn't mean they buy anything.' I bought a bag of bad-for-you caramels instead.

On the road to Halifax, the Lookoff gave wide peaceful views over the Annapolis Valley's patchwork farms. An inventive suitor had tilled 'Lise Marry Me' many metres long in the soil. Her reply went unrecorded.

Henry Wadsworth Longfellow's poem 'Evangeline' told another love story, an Acadian Romeo and Juliet saga. This part of the Nova Scotia coast was Evangeline country. In Longfellow's poem the fictitious Acadian heroine Evangeline, booted out of Nova Scotia in the great expulsion, wandered to Louisiana searching for her lost love. Of course it all ended in tears for everybody.

At Grand Pré a national monument marked the spot of the Acadian expulsion. But after the historical village and cow bingo, how could other Acadian attractions compare? They couldn't. We drove on to Halifax.

Time did not allow a Nova Scotia circumnavigation. We settled on a plan for a short cruise from our Halifax motel along the South Shore to the rum-running village of Lunenburg, then a zip across to Cape Breton for a tiki tour on the way to the Newfoundland ferry. But first, a date with a rooster.

'You've got to take that car to the Chickenburger,' a fellow motel guest told us. 'It's not far from here.'

Before A&W, he said, there was the Chickenburger diner, opened for business in 1940 and, amazingly, not yet steamrollered by fast-food chains. The trademark rooster atop the diner flashed its fluorescent tail feathers as only a 1940s neon rooster could. We ordered at the outside counter then took the chookburgers inside and ate them from pressed-paper trays under a dazzling purple-and-yellow Jetson-style neon dome.

This was classic-car country. The Beast shared parking space with some old-time Chickenburger regulars. The car owners talked about gas mileage. What the cars talked about, I could only guess. The Beast didn't yet know about its new life in Okotoks.

The highway from Halifax to Lunenburg wended along a coast of weathered fishing shacks, lobster traps in stacks and glacial boulders tossed up from the last ice age bald as shaved mammoth rumps. At Prospect, Ken pulled in to a grassy picnic spot down an overgrown lane, the better to walk on the rumpy rocks and gaze at the sea. On our return a frowning old Prospectian stood writing down the Beast's licence number.

'Hello? Is there a problem?'

'You're trespassing. You're on private land.'

'Sorry. We didn't know. There wasn't a sign. Sorry. We're leaving now.'

The Prospectian ignored these apologies. With a stab of the pen he finished recording the evidence and stomped off down the lane. I wondered whether to alert Bruce to be on the lookout for a trespass notice but decided, no. He'd probably flee to Cuba.

A smattering of shanties clung to chunks of grey rock at Peggy's Cove. The village's sum total of sixty locals didn't seem to mind the thousands of tourists slipping and sliding over their patch photographing one of Canada's most photographed lighthouses and politely applauding a bagpiper bleating on a rock in front of a lighthouse. One of the sixty was a retired cod and pollock fisherman. He liked our car. He had a '58 Chevy two-door once.

'Hurricane Juan blew the shed down but didn't touch the car.'

Shrouded in good old hurricane-resistant General Motors metal – excepting the wipers, of course – we headed down the scraped-bare highway. Near Peggy's Cove a simple granite memorial to Swissair Flight 111 overlooked the aeroplane-swallowing waters of St Margaret's Bay. The doomed plane and its passengers fell flaming out of the sky into the sea nearly a decade earlier, killing all 229 on board. One of the St Margaret's Bay locals told us they'd picked up burnt dinner trays and other grisly wreckage for years. It wasn't the way these kindly coastal folk liked to receive visitors, and not something they ever wanted to see again.

Needing a little pick-me-up after that bit of grimness we pulled up just past Seabright at Fredie's Fantastic Fish House. From inside a kennel-sized trailer, box-of-birds Tammy Frederick and her mother served up fat juicy fillets of haddock in crispy batter and hand-cut fries with, yum, the skin still on. Tammy went one-up on chocolate fish: she handed out chocolate lobsters on a stick as an end-of-season treat for her regulars, and for us too, even though we weren't regulars. We would've been, but for the small problem of distance.

After Fox Pen Road we tootled along past Puddle Hill Road to

Queensland Beach. After so much New Zealandness, here was an Aussie connection. The white sand and blue sea could have been at a beach in Australia, except the water was freeze-yer-bits-off frigid and there wasn't a shark in sight.

Along the twisty turns of the Aspotogan Peninsula the seaweed swirled over the rocks in long hairy mats. It looked like herds of seafaring yaks had beached themselves. But it was a peaceful and pretty place. A line of perky fishing dories at a speck called Northwest Cove showed the region's true colours, and almost all were primaries. Fishing boats at anchor, dories and shacks – all red and yellow, green and blue. I hailed a pair of fishermen aboard the boat *All Three*. Lorraine Boutilier and his son Blaine (if there was someone else making up 'all three' I didn't find out who it was) were sorting their trap nets to go bluefin tuna fishing.

'Could get one or twenty-one,' said Lorraine, laconic as fisherfolk the world over. 'Could be two hundred or a thousand pounds.'

At East River's St George's Anglican Church one red tree flamed over grassy graves of other once-were locals: the long-gone Cooks, the apparently Frails, the no longer Fleets. This single tree hinted at a winter that, so far, was slow to come.

One Cook still above ground was Fred. Fred collected hub caps. Ken nosed the Chevy down the lane for a look at the fifty or so shiny discs nailed to Fred's shed.

'I've lived here all my life,' said humble Fred. He found the hub caps at yard sales and sold them to passers-by for 'mebbee fifty cents or a dollar apiece. Sometimes they want one that fell off an old car going by and I picked it up.'

The oldest was from a '58 Volkswagen. A short scouting around didn't turn up any for the Chevy and really, hub caps were one thing the Chevy didn't need, despite what Bruce thought.

The drive to Lunenburg was taking much longer than we'd planned. But that was the pleasure of cruising across a country in your own car. Buses had their place as emergency transport when the car broke down far from anywhere. Hitchhiking did too, in countries with pleasant scenery, gentle climates and a dearth of bloodsucking insects or murderous transients, if the hitchhiker had scads of time and did his bit by entertaining the driver. Having our own set of wheels meant freedom of time and place, of course within the limits of an old car's foibles.

Lunenburg we liked. The town, a UNESCO world heritage site, was awash with the restored Victorian charm of widow's walks atop houses of blue, pink and white reposing on leafy cobbled streets. Out of the handsome red boat-building sheds on the town's waterfront sailed Canada's most famous racing schooner, the *Bluenose*. The 1921 schooner so soundly whipped its New England rivals the grateful Canadian government immortalised it on the back of the Canadian ten-cent coin, the dime. You couldn't get more famous than that, except if you were a loon.

Aboard the replica *Bluenose II* bobbing at the wharf a swarm of eager young sailors polished brass, furled sails, swabbed decks. I asked one of them if he was descended from rum runners. He blushed and denied it.

During Prohibition in the US in the 1920s, opportunistic Lunenburgers found gainful employment smuggling liquor in schoonerloads to the US, from the Caribbean or from the French-held islands of St Pierre and Miquelon near Newfoundland. The ships scooted down the eastern seaboard's Rum Row, unloading it by the caseload to such heavyweights as Al Capone, who kept himself in handguns and villainous hats by on-selling the booze to thirsty Americans.

For old times' sake we downed a tot of rum at a seafarer's tavern and reminisced about the good old smuggling days we'd never had. Then, in a seaside town heaving with fish dinners, I pined for a burger. At Large Marge's Diner jukebox tunes played four for a quarter, there were Big Fella burgers on the grill and coconut cream pie for afters. The waitress showed off her tattoos and said she didn't know for sure, but she thought Large Marge was a trucker gal. Large Marge could be forgiven that little lapse; the place was a classic.

Down at the infamous bootlegger's waterfront our own classic attracted a respectful evening crowd.

'Is that a '56? I had a '55 Buick once.'

Soon we'd be whistling that same sorry tune.

All kinds of cargo came and went on the docks at Halifax. I was morbidly fascinated by one of the most gruesome: the *Titanic*'s dead. We found Fairview Lawn Cemetery on the map and for a contemplative hour or so strolled the sorrowful headstones. One of the inscriptions on the dozens of monuments, all dated that fateful 15 April 1912, was to one of the 'heroic crew' who 'showed once more to all the world how Englishmen should die'. The monument didn't say how, precisely, Englishmen should die, but standing manfully on the deck of a sinking ship, not scrambling overtop of women and children to get to the lifeboats, was no doubt the way to do it.

Many of the drowned were women and children on their way to a new life with fathers and husbands already hard at work in the new country. The stuffed bunny rabbits, teddy bears and toys at the grave of the 'Unknown child' showed that somebody still cared about these long-lost souls.

The day of our own Atlantic voyage, on the Newfoundland ferry, drew near. The trip from North Sydney to Argentia in eastern Newfoundland had a reputation for pounding even strong-stomached sailors into hollow-eyed retching wrecks. Some wit once said, 'The only thing that keeps you alive when you're seasick is the hope you're going to die soon.' I knew that state very well. The indelicate roadside spewing problem of my youth still plagued me, not only in cars (except, oddly enough, the Beast) but also in tiny aeroplanes and most boats, even docked ones – although none of Canada's ferries had done me in so far.

The worst voyage I'd ever suffered was a three-hour ferry ride from the Greek island of Symi, a blip in the Mediterranean Sea, to the larger island of Rhodes. The sea, a placid thing on the journey over, grew enough muscles on the way back to punch the skinny little ferry all over the ring for many rounds. Passengers on the top deck hurled their lunch onto lower-deck passengers, who in turn hurled theirs on their feet. I crawled off the boat in Rhodes, fell to my knees and delivered my own lunch to ungrateful passers-by, swearing never to leave dry land again.

Moving to sea-girt New Zealand hadn't done a thing for my prairie stomach. Still, a couple of days, part of Cape Breton Island and a previous life as a pharmacist stood between the Newfoundland ferry ride and more such public humiliation.

Old Brian from the Lake Huron *Chi-Cheemaun* ferry had done a good job of selling Cape Breton Island. We could only see a wee piece of it, but ceilidhs figured big in the plan – a bit of fiddling and jigging, a pint of Guinness and, with a bit of luck, no bagpipes. Maybe another moose.

Maybe not. The moose of eastern Canada proved even more elusive than the moose of British Columbia. Either they'd learned, or there were none left to learn, about the dangers of roads. Near Halifax at Cow Bay, a pleasingly lifelike giant moose, erected in 1959 according to a Friends of the Moose plaque, posed for photos in a rubbish-blown car park. I hoped this lonely old Cow Bay moose wasn't the last we'd see.

In Halifax Ken readied the Beast for the final days of its adventure; washed its face, brushed its grinning grille, checked the tyres for tread, the oil for oiliness, the wipers for wiping strength, which they'd regained all on their own. Then we set course across Nova Scotia's mid-quarters over the Canso Causeway, up the Ceilidh Trail, the Scottish towns of Creignish, Craigmore, Campbell all blurs in the rear-view mirror, and burst through the doors of the Red Shoe Inn at Mabou under a chorus line of red shoes hanging from the roof.

'Looks like dancing to me,' said Ken.

'Yes, but there's also good Nova Scotia beer and music. You'll like it.'

An inn full of jig-dancers and Guinness-drinkers had the same idea of how to while away a Sunday afternoon. There was standing room only, and then only for thin folk stacked in sideways. For this was no ordinary ceilidh. The sister part of Canada's famous singing siblings, the Rankin Family, owned the Red Shoe Inn. Punters coming to hear the fiddler, guitarist and pianist trio rip out a 'Tripper's Jig' or maybe 'Little Donald in the Pig Pen' hoped the Rankin sisters would get up to a little musical something too.

We invaded a square of space at a table with some toe-tapping American Rankin fans who'd driven up from Vermont expressly to visit this pub. Cape Breton dancing, unlike the Wanuskewin circle dance, was not a sport for amateurs. Teenagers, mothers, grandfathers in jeans and baseball caps, all capered about drumming dents in the wooden floor, cheering slapping clapping. Outside, a schoolboy tap-danced up and down the steps. They couldn't help themselves. These were bred-in-the-bone jiggers. So too were the Rankin sisters, Heather, Raylene, Cookie and Genevieve, who not only sang like reincarnated songbirds, they shook a shapely leg too.

Heather stopped by for a breather.

'The former owner of the inn was a well-known fiddler, he played a tune called "Red Shoes". Now people mail us stinky old red shoes from all over.'

For anyone missing their own family or Mom's home cooking the Red Shoe Inn made a fine stand-in. This was a family affair. Heather and her sisters came from a family of twelve – a typical Cape Breton family, just like Old Brian had said. In honour of Raylene's birthday all of the pub patrons joined in a Happy Birthday singalong and a slice of birthday fruitcake.

'Here,' said Heather, 'have some to fatten you up.'

Just like being at home.

On the other side of Cape Breton at the seaside town of Baddeck, Ken, who's fond of a good invention, went off to the Alexander Graham Bell Museum to learn about the fine mind that gave the world the forebears of the Cellphone That Never Rang. I went off to check for emails and buy a replacement pair of sunglasses for the lost pair I later found staring at me from the Beast's dashboard. Joggers old and young hustling down Baddeck's main street had just finished the twenty-fifth anniversary run for the Terry Fox Marathon of Hope. There was nothing from Bruce, but I took the marathon as a hopeful sign that all would be well for man, woman and Beast.

If Cod Tongues
Could Talk

' Oi loiks auld cairs. '

Classic-car fan, Newfoundland

Newfoundland. A giant lump of ship-wrecking rock, far adrift in a bad-tempered sea.

'I think Newfoundland invented the wind,' mused a chap leaning on the ferry rail, watching seagulls ride the thermals.

By some massive stroke of luck the sea was in an affable mood, the infamous Cabot Strait as flat and innocent as a large blue tiddlywink. We'd boarded the North Sydney ferry at some dim hour of the morning, armed to the eyebrows with anti-seasickness pills, water, snacks and warm windproof jackets. The crossing to Argentia on the Avalon Peninsula, said the ferry crew, took fourteen hours. Fourteen whole hours, about the same as crossing from Italy to Greece.

The Beast shared cosy – too cosy for my paranoid liking – deck space with big-bumpered SUVs plus Porsches and Studebakers bound for the Targa Newfoundland road rally. Now that the Beast was nearly sold I fretted ridiculously about damaging it. I imagined the SUV behind the Beast rocking into it on a wave and taking out the tailgate. Maybe we should duct tape the pillows and duvets over the tail lights in case of a spontaneous demolition derby?

'You're a crazy woman,' said Ken, unfeelingly but accurately. 'Stop worrying.' If the Targa rally drivers entrusted their expensive rare autos to the Newfoundland ferry workers, so could we.

Aboard the MV *Joseph and Clara Smallwood* all was serene. Fittingly, our first-ever trip to Newfoundland had begun on a ferry named for the Newfoundland premier (and his wife) who manhandled Britain's oldest colony into the bosom of Canada – when Canada joined Newfoundland, as Newfoundlanders liked to remember it – a scant fifty-six years earlier. On the sheltered decks brave passengers stripped down to bikinis and shorts. When the wind picked up we staked out some comfy recliner chairs and watched movies regularly interrupted by the crew reminding passengers that the ice-cream kiosk was now open (and closed), the cafeteria was now open (and closed), and not to forget to see the Cod Kings now playing traditional tunes in the lounge. Happy thirtieth anniversary to Fred and Judy. But for the lack of all-you-can-eat buffet dinners, it felt like a low-budget cruise.

First impression of Newfoundland: where was it? The ferry docked in darkness deep and black enough to hide thirty types of sin. Undaunted, the Targa cars roared off and vanished. The feeble beam from the Beast's headlights merely bounced off this treacly treachery. If there'd been a moose on the road two moose paces away we wouldn't have seen it.

Newfoundlanders called moose the 'Newfoundland speed bump'. More than five hundred moose got into messes with cars on Newfoundland roads every year. This I read in the *Gulf News* on the ferry. In the latest moose-car accident, 'there was no report of personal injury'. To the motorist, I guessed. The moose wasn't available for comment. Another true moose moment would be welcome, but not of the close-encounter-in-the-dark kind.

Argentia offered not much more than a tourist information centre and its car park. The village of Placentia further along the road had a B&B, we were told, but it was full. On our first Newfoundland evening we slept in a tourist information centre car park, and counted ourselves lucky.

In the morning the blackness shrank away like an exorcised ghoul and a cottony fog barged in. Still no sign of Newfoundland, save for the couple of metres of road in front of the Beast's bumper, but it had to be there somewhere.

An hour later the fog peeled back. Newfoundland, on first glimpse, made Scotland look tropical. The trees had hitched up their skirts and taken off for balmier climes. But there was a bleak moorish charm to the scurvy shrubs and determined mosses scrimmaging over the rocks.

At the Cape St Mary's gannet colony the park ranger handed over a pamphlet about the birds and said, 'It's a twanny minnit waack.'

'Sorry?'

'It's a twanny minnit waack,' he repeated helpfully, pointing to a path along the cliff.

The ranger had heard about New Zealand's Cape Kidnappers gannet colony. He knew the difference between northern and southern birds.

'Blaack tayle fedders fer ye, whaayte tayle fedders fer we.'

The path skirted a high cliff, dropping to a sea the colour of fog. The gannets did smelly birdy things, shrieking and preening their white tail feathers and showing other birds what flying really meant. Then the sea, the sky and the path along the hundred-metre cliffs all turned the colour of fog. Tripping over sheep poop I was relieved it wasn't a terty minnit waack back to the car. The pamphlet said, quite firmly, 'Stay on the path.' This, and the creeping spooky fogginess, brought to mind the scene in the movie *American Werewolf in London* where the hero does *not* stay on the path, to his bitter and hairy regret. It was the sheep's job to cry werewolf. I hoped they knew that.

At the village of Branch, horses grazing in a marsh made a pretty, bucolic scene. A woman out walking stopped to watch us take photos. For a full ten minutes she chatted gaily away at a machine-gun rate while we nodded and smiled. Then 'Oi'll be off, my darlings,' she cried, and walked on.

'What did she say?' gasped Ken, who'd barely recovered from having to speak French in Québec.

'I'm not sure. Something about potholes being haird on the cairs.' (She was right. A Targa rally driver later told us one of the Porsches fell in a pothole and cracked in half, breaking both the driver's legs.)

Canadian friends had warned us, with glee, to brush up on the Newfoundland accent. How hard could it be? They spoke English, didn't they? Well, no. In this part of Newfoundland it was all Irish to us. French, Spanish, Portuguese and Basques all sailed to Newfoundland waters through five centuries, seeking fish-shaped gold: cod. Irish seamen jumping British ships in Newfoundland laid down the language. In parts of Newfoundland the dialect cobbled together sixteenth-century Irish and a little of everything else picked up along the way. But not everyone spoke it. There was no way of telling if you were in line for a verbal machine-gunning until it was too late.

We slalomed the potholed road to St John's on a coast fraught with history. Wireless operators at Cape Race on the tip of the Avalon Peninsula were the first to receive the doomed *Titanic*'s distress signal. The pilgrim ship, the *Mayflower*, called in up the coast at Renews in 1620, before sailing to Plymouth Rock in New England. Basque whalers and fishers mooched into the protected harbour at Ferryland in the fifteenth century, well before the French and English started one of their infernal scraps over it.

St John's was a rollicking old town bright with wooden houses lined up in a flurry of pastel colours and chaotic with interesting flotsam and jetsam, both breathing and not. Here, 989 accordionists playing 'Mussels in the Corner' had recently squeezed out a new record for the most accordions ever played at once. Another disappointing near-miss in a long list of things we almost saw. On Water Street a bleached blonde sexagenarian in tiny shorts and a halter top shouted, 'I'll break your friggin' head' to no one in particular, a few metres down from a blind-from-birth guitarist lamenting lost love, Jimmy Reeves style.

A backpacker couple tailed by Brandy the happy black dog importuned passers-by for a penny a poem. I had the guilty feeling this was the hitchhiking couple and dog trio we'd bypassed on the Terry Fox Courage Highway, so the poem, something short and sharp about love and hate, earned more loonies than pennies. Who gave rides to people with dogs? Animal lovers and truck drivers, said the girl. Except when the dog got sprayed by a skunk.

We recharged ourselves at a family-run restaurant promising real Newfoundland home cooking.

'What'll ye be having, my darlings?' asked the motherly waitress in a café all a-frill with gingham. So charming was she I'd have happily eaten fried boot soles.

The closest thing to boot soles on the menu was Newfoundland Steak – my old nemesis, fried bologna. I ordered cod tongues and scrunchions. These came with a quick lesson in the three rules of real Newfoundland home cooking: there must be cod, or parts thereof, on every plate. The deep-fryer was Queen of the Kitchen. Vegetables must be punished.

I stabbed a medallion of cod tongue (actually the throat, I was told, and not the part a cod would speak with if only it had something to say), topped it with a scrunchion of shrivelled salt pork and deemed it chewy, salty and oily. Ken ate his deep-fried cod and pale frayed carrot with the haunted look of a fresh fruit and salad addict sentenced to life with deathless vegetables.

In the morning we drove under gathering clouds to the lighthouse at Cape Spear near St John's. Cape Spear marked the geographical end of the line, the most easterly point in North America for us and the Beast. From here the track led west across Newfoundland, then across the Cabot Strait again and back to Halifax. There we had a plane to catch. In the meantime there were people to meet and cod to eat, although much less of it than in olden golden times.

Cod built Newfoundland but, it was said, pillaging offshore trawlers pulled the cod out from Newfoundlanders. Since the Canadian government closed down virtually all of the industry in 1992, Newfoundlanders had grieved.

At the Cape Spear lighthouse three old codgers, bent like shepherd's crooks into the wind, clutched beers and jostled each other in the jovial way of old mates well met. They'd fished the cod. They hadn't seen each other for twenty years.

One of the friends, a jolly soul in jaunty white hat, said, 'If I jump in that sea and catch a fish in me arms it's an eight hundrit dollar fine. That's a large price for a fish.'

His friends nodded.

'Ah, well, it's a lovely auld day. The guvmint can cancel the fishing, but they can't cancel the weather.'

'They can tax it,' said Ken, still smarting from GST and PST and environmental tax and the inflationary price of the great outdoors.

The three old friends liked that a lot. Jaunty White Hat said, 'That'll be in the next budget. In this one cigarettes are going up ten cents. That's a large price for cigarettes. They'd better make them an inch longer.' Then he told a joke, not about cod, but about something else dear to their hearts. It went like this.

A Torontonian, a Nova Scotian and an old Newfie went into a bar and each ordered a beer. Each found a fly in their beer.

The Torontonian looked in his beer and said, 'Hey bartender! I have a fly in my beer. Give me another beer.'

The Nova Scotian looked in his beer, found the fly, picked it out and continued drinking.

The old Newfie looked in his beer, saw the fly, grabbed it by the wings, shook it over the glass and yelled, 'Spit it out!'

Now that was a good joke. The old friends sucked on the last of their beer and tootled back down the hill to see what the wives might be brewing up for lunch.

Atop Signal Hill on the other side of St John's, Marconi received the first transatlantic signal: Morse code for the letter 'S'. After digesting this singular piece of history I took a last look at the city's wooden houses tipping downhill to the sea. Ken had an earnest word with the Beast about staying out of potholes. Then we pointed west to see how Newfoundlanders were keeping mind and body together in these codless times.

The map of Newfoundland read like an old mariner's saga: Cuckold's Cove Road, Seal Cove, Chapel's Cove, Gallows Cove, Cupids, Harbour Grace, Conception Harbour. Bareneed, Bishop's Cove, Bristol's Hope, Heart's Content, Heart's Desire, Heart's Delight. Hopeall. An impassioned epic of love, betrayal and sorrow, death and the sea, missing nothing but verbs.

Outside Seal Cove a tree hung with dented baking pans and rusty cheese graters stood outside a garage-cum-shop. Every item inside the shop dangled from the ceiling by a gold ribbon.

'I don't like bare,' said the proprietor, a chunky guy in a 'Canada' baseball cap.

Bare the shop was not. To navigate from one end to the other I dodged dishes, cavorted amongst candlestick holders, danced with doorknobs. Amongst all that bounty I managed to buy not so much as a doily.

Tiny, cute as a bug's ear Brigus up from Gallows Cove, down from Cupids and tucked in a saucer-sized cove, should have been a well-kept secret. It wasn't. Captain Bob Bartlett, the ice pilot who guided explorer Peary almost to the North Pole, was born in this town of wooden houses built on walls of slate by canals; tourists came to see his house. Movie stars dropped in too, if not to see Captain Bob's birthplace then to eat some of Esther Spracklin's home baking, according to Esther Spracklin. At the end of the last road before the sea, at a house busy with more lawn ornaments than in all of New Brunswick, Esther baked blueberry pies, partridgeberry pies, bakeapple tarts, raisin scones and strudel in her own kitchen, a sort of Boulangerie Esther.

Actors Daniel Radcliffe (Harry Potter) and Meg Ryan had come for a visit one day.

'They sat on my porch for hours, and sang and danced to traditional Newfoundland music. Meg Ryan forgot her purse and I had to run down the road with it. Some people said I should sell the carpet they stood on on eBay for five thousand dollars. Denzel Washington came here too. He's gorgeous. Tall, dark. When people heard about it some women came and rubbed their breasts on the banister where he'd been leaning. It's sick what some people get up to.'

She paused just long enough for us to wish her well with her online transaction, buy an Esther Spracklin's blueberry pie and retreat to a tiny, cute as a bug's ear café.

'What's a touton?' I asked the waitress, giving the word a French sound. 'The menu says baked beans and toutons.'

'Oh, that's tawt'ns, lovey. That's fried bread.'

I had fishcakes. Ken, grasping for vegetables, ordered pea and ham soup and a beer.

'Beer is not a vegetable,' I observed.

'In Newfoundland it is,' said Ken.

We ate Esther's pie in our tiny, cute as a bug's ear B&B on the edge of the harbour, quacked at by ducks who sounded as if they'd had Esther's pie before, and wouldn't mind seconds.

The next day the unusually benign weather fled west. The wipers laboured to clear a lashing rain ominously similar to Hurricane Katrina's tail. Struggling to see through a blurry windscreen, Ken sat forward, nose pressed nearly against the glass.

'Can you see anything on your side?' he said.

'Not much, what about you?'

'Not much.'

We all took a short rest at Harbour Grace, where, one imagined, Amelia Earhart enjoyed better weather when she set out from here on her solo flight across the Atlantic seventy-odd years earlier. It was almost windy enough to open the car doors and fly the Beast.

Few folk shared the road on this Sunday morning – likely they were all at church or at home sleeping off a night out on the vegetables. The only other wheeled thing on the road was a metal pie plate. It broke out of the roadside scrub and rolled on its edge down the centre line for hundreds of metres. We watched, cheering it on, till the bullying wind snatched it up and clanged it into the leaning scrub.

The wipers grumped, thumped—

'Oh no.'

Grumped, thumped—

'Feck!' said Ken, furiously twiddling the wiper knob.

And died.

We'd been driving through a small town. Ken pulled into the nearest car park, popped the bonnet, dropped it again, splashed back into the car.

'Where are we?'

I consulted the map. 'We passed Carbonear and Victoria so it must be Heart's Content.'

'You're joking.'

'No, have a look. Heart's Content.'

We sat in the Beast wondering what to do next, our hearts sorely discontented.

'What is this place we're sitting outside?' I asked eventually.

'It says Heart's Content Cable Station.'

Neither of us knew what a cable station was, but it was open and looked more enthralling than sitting in a car in the rain. The cable station, it transpired, was a museum. The museum attendant hanging up our dripping jackets tut-tutted in sympathy when Ken mentioned the wiper problem.

'Nobody here can fix them, it's a Sunday anyway. There might be somebody in Carbonear.'

That meant backtracking. For the time being we were going nowhere but inside the dry warm museum, which, for a big old building filled top to bottom with incomprehensible electrical gadgets, was surprisingly engrossing. The very first transatlantic telegraph cable laid along the seabed from Ireland landed at Heart's Content in 1866, after several foiled attempts when the cable broke mid-ocean. Transatlantic telegrams did not come cheap: twenty words cost twenty pounds sterling in gold. The sender chose their words carefully.

The boat that laid the cable, the *Great Eastern*, at the time the largest boat afloat on any sea, was built to give the passenger clippers sailing to the South Pacific a run for their money. But when the Suez Canal opened, the *Great Eastern* became a giant white elephant. The ship didn't fit through the canal. Hence life as a transatlantic cable layer.

The rain slowed to a drizzle, so we set out once more into the wind. The wipers airily behaved as if nothing untoward had happened. At Heart's Desire the wind drew breath and blew the sea into crests of amber foaming against a coast sharp with rocks. Tree branches semaphored distress signals. In the whipping grass seagulls bunked down, beaks to the wind – there'd be no flying in this weather. Further along, Heart's Delight did not. We carried on to Dildo, where a local shrugged his shoulders at the obvious question.

'Oi don't knows 'bout dat off de bat.'

Dildos as the modern world knew them hadn't been invented when the town was named, but, the local said, 'dere's sure been some fun since den, aye b'ye.'

The bad weather beat us into the shelter of a B&B next to the harbour. Camping was out for now, indeed as far as I was concerned, for the rest of the trip.

Shakespeare's *A Winter's Tale* mentioned 'delicate burdens of dildos and fadings', explained a pamphlet in our room. In any case the locals liked the name, whatever it meant, and weren't about to change it. Strewn around the bottom of a cove, the fishing village deserved a sweeter name, maybe Heart's Delight.

I peered inside a boatshed and saw a seal skeleton in pieces. Seals, said the young woman attending our B&B, floated down on ice pans. There were sealskin boots and mitts, slick as spun silver, for sale at the B&B. A stuffed seal pup lolled in the hallway.

Through the years the Newfoundland sealers had suffered the world's wrath. In New Zealand, Ken, who'd never been near a seal in his life, much less molested one, was once or twice called a 'seal basher'. But the seals suffered a lesser fate than the Newfoundland aborigines, the Beothuks, whose story was soberly reported in the Dildo Interpretation Centre. The marauding English and French massacred some of them; disease got the rest. The last remaining Beothuk died of tuberculosis in the 1820s. It wasn't, as Newfoundlanders said, de proper ting.

The next day the Trans-Canada, in its true state as Highway 1, finally snared us. Highway 1 was the only road to the Bonavista Peninsula. But in this part of Canada it was a benign thing, only lightly trafficked, and a quick way to travel north, past Come By Chance and Goobies, on to the Clarenville turn-off to Trinity. The town entranced at first glance, even more bewitching than Brigus or Dildo or any of the other sweet places on this route. Coloured boxes of houses stood proud around a perfect cove, a lighthouse blinked at the end of a long curved finger of land.

A painting on the wall of our B&B depicted an iceberg sailing past the town like a giant's tricorner hat skimming the sea. At the craft shop the woman on the desk said, 'There were only a hundred icebergs came down this way this year. It could be global warming. Are you on your own, honey?'

'No,' I said, 'my husband's outside, waiting on the bench.'

'He wouldn't come into a craft shop, would he. That's why I have the bench outside, for husbands.'

Further up the road, at Cape Bonavista, it was hard to believe anything remotely warm was going on anywhere. On this lonely point John Cabot (really the Italian Giovanni Caboto, pitching for another side) claimed Newfoundland, Terra Nova, Terreneuve, for Henry VII of England. In school assembly we'd raised our little kid voices to sing the Canadianised version of the Woody Guthrie folk song:

This land is your land, this land is my land
From Bonavista to Vancouver Island
From the Arctic Circle to the Great Lakes waters
This land was made for you and me.

I'd never known where Bonavista was. Now I did. It was the windiest place on earth, windier even than the Arctic Circle. I winched myself out of the Beast, staggered up the hill to the famous explorer's statue and a candy-cane striped lighthouse, stumbled headlong into a patch of burnt-ochre heather and ruby-red partridgeberries (very pretty seen at such close range), declared I'd seen enough and retreated to the car.

'That wind'll rip the hair out of your nostrils,' said a fellow sheltering behind his van. 'That's quite the old buggy you've got. Did you really drive it all the way from Saskatchewan?'

I described our Beast's journey.

'Git away,' he said. 'That's a fair distance for an old car.' The Beast bent into a little bow. Or maybe it was only the wind knocking it to its knees.

This was no place to dally. It was time to refuel selves and Beast. At Newman's Cove the grocery store sold forty-eight kinds of biscuits but not a single fresh thing. In what may not have been a coincidence, they also sold headstones. We ate biscuits.

Since that initial shock rise in New Brunswick, petrol prices had settled at just over $1.30 per litre. At a petrol pump on Route 230, close to not very much at all, an old guy in a blue flannel shirt stared open-mouthed at the petrol nozzle sticking out of the tail light.

'If I'se never seed it I'se never would believed it,' he said, shaking his head. 'I'se seed it all, now.'

The petrol cost thirty-five dollars.

'That's how much it cost us to go from Saskatoon to Vancouver Island and back in my diesel Volkswagen Rabbit,' Ken reminisced.

'That was over twenty-five years ago,' I reminded him.

No one could call the Beast economical, even twenty-five years ago. But it was a sight classier than a Volkswagen Rabbit.

As we entered Terra Nova National Park a sign tallied the

moose-car accident rate: six so far this year. Where was this plethora of moose? Not one moose had crossed our path in this moose-plagued province.

We flapped into Gander to rest from the wearying wind. For a long time the town of Gander was barely a town. It was an airport, the biggest in the world when the first plane arrived at the beginning of World War II, with a bit o' town tacked on. It still didn't appeal at first glance, though the flying Targa rally drivers soon arrived to liven up the streets.

At our B&B another guest had undertaken an epic journey of his own. The man from Abbotsford had driven his giant-pumpkin sized Mercedes Smart Car from British Columbia to Newfoundland. The three-cylinder, 0.8-litre car ran on the smell of an oily rag, getting 81 miles to the gallon (3.5 litres per 100 kilometres). Sometimes it was much as 100 miles. The whole journey cost $550 in petrol.

The driver's mission was to alert Canadians to gas-gobbling's effect on the planet. It was, no one can deny, an environmentally unfriendly thing to drive an old V8 across an entire nation. So far the Beast had guzzled about five times more of the earth's resources than the Smart Car. But even as I agreed this was a worthy thing to do, I doubted that crowds of folk came up to him to reminisce about the good times they'd had in their own economical compacts.

At Twillingate, a wander north of Gander, we lunched at a fish market on Shoal Tickle, past Herring Neck. In a land once so thick with fish 'you could walk on the backs of them', we dined once again on burgers.

'What's not deep fried?' asked Ken, ever hopeful.

'There's hamburgers.'

'Not deep fried? In a bun, and everything?'

'Yes,' said the puzzled girl at the counter.

It wasn't a silly question. In a particularly ghastly example of Scottish cuisine on the European Ford trip, I'd ordered a hamburger at a takeaway bar in a northern Scottish town. Ken inexplicably ordered haggis. Both arrived deep fried, the hamburger greasy in a paper sleeve, not a bun in sight, bare of any condiment. We chucked out the lot and drove straight to France.

'Just checking,' said Ken. 'I'll have the hamburger.'

'What's fish and brewis?' I asked.

'Oh, that's salt cod boiled up with potatoes and bread, that's the brewis. Then you add scrunchions for flavour.'

'I'll have the hamburger,' I said.

'If I see another vegetable I'm going to take a photo of it,' said Ken.

On the harbour a little museum stood at the end of a wharf, or 'stage'. Melvin Horwood, a 'forcibly retired cod fisherman', showed us rocks painted with pictures and stories, books on cod, fishing lines. He spoke about the lost cod like the death of a close friend, with palpable sorrow. Now he fished for squid and snow crab, pegging up squid like laundry on a line.

'Fishing is something natural, it's instinctive. I had a healthy lifestyle on the water. Using a handline, it was so exciting. You didn't know if the fish was going to be six inches or three feet long. Some cod weighed eighty pounds, the record for here is a hundred and two pounds. But the nets killed the fisheries. There's still some cod, they fish for it in West Newfoundland. Now there's ten million seals eating the cod. But around here we can't take one fish for ourselves.'

The gargantuan cod might be gone but the icebergs still came in the spring. There was a whole language for icebergs: slob ice (thick slush with ice in it), small icebergs called bergy bits, and growlers, those dangerous low-riding shipwreckers. The bergs calved off Greenland and floated down the Labrador Current. Some were a hundred thousand tonnes. Some showed up with seal hitchhikers.

'The bergs can sit in the harbour for a couple of weeks before moving on,' said Melvin.

That, I said, was something I'd really like to see.

Melvin handed me a card. 'Give me a call before you come and I'll tell you if there are any bergs. I can see them from my window. I don't even need to get out of bed.'

Near Badger a truck carrying a bodiless moose head peering skyward in surprise passed us at speed. Further along, behind a line of pick-up trucks parked by the side of the road, four extra-large, moose-sized body bags hung in the trees like a spider's breakfast. So that's where the moose had gone – either in body bags or retreated to the safety of national parks.

Gros Morne National Park, deep with fiords, was as stunning a place as you'd find anywhere. At least that was how it looked in the brochure. Solid fog smothered the park down to our ankles, where little could be seen except a boardwalk snaking through an arthritic tuckamore forest, and everywhere signs of moose. Moose poop, moose hoof prints, all fresh, but no moose. In nearby Trout River the moose were eating apples off the trees, said a mechanic admiring the Beast in the car park. The apple tree owners called the RCMP to shoo them off.

Ken pleaded for one last round of camping in the Beast, since the rain had stopped. The car's final camping spot overlooked a finger bay at Loch Lomond, near a meadow known to be frequented by moose. 'Ye sees dem at noight,' said another camper.

A skulk around the moose meadow turned up only moose bones. But even without moose, this was still a moose moment. A titan sun burned a hole in the dusk. The night was still and warm. We sat around a campfire drinking partridgeberry wine bought for just such a special occasion. The flames flared orange on the Beast's creamy rump.

'Oi loiks auld cairs,' said a classic car lover walking down the lane. I had to agree.

Highway 1 ran down to Port aux Basques, where the ferry left for the seven-hour trip back to North Sydney. Port aux Basques bustled with people coming and going. Our ferry didn't leave till the next day. On our last night in Newfoundland we could do better than this. So we did. A small road took us past Margaree, Fox Roost, Isle aux Morts, past still lily ponds, ferns stuck like feathers in the dunes, to Rose Blanche and the end of the road. Outports further along could be reached only by ferry.

And here we found the best of the best. Rose Blanche was

prettier than Trinity or Twillingate. The houses clambered up and down boulders of granite, snug up against small wharves painted in matching colours nudging the water. The fog rolled in. We trawled a path along the sea past black dogs and yellow dogs, laundry snapping on lines. The fog rolled out.

'This is the prettiest place we've seen in Newfoundland,' I remarked to a man walking a wooden door down the road.

''Tis,' he agreed. 'But there's no work for the young ones. They go to Alberta or BC to work in the oilfields. Some of them come back. A lot don't. One day there'll be no one left in Rose Blanche.'

At a seaside café hung with fishing nets, rods and hand-made model boats we ate our last Newfoundland supper: fried cod and cod tongues, shrimp and scallops, mashed spuds and gravy, watery but welcome coleslaw; partridgeberry pie for pudding.

The waitress said, 'There's a hurricane coming. Ophelia, this one's called.'

My stomach, full of deep-fried sea creatures, rolled in and out like fog. 'Do you think the ferry will sail tomorrow?'

'Oh, she'll sail. But if it's the *Leif Ericson* don't get on her, my darlings. She rolls terrible. No, you don't want that boat.'

She phoned the ferry company.

'They say it's the *Caribou*, not that old tub. Should be all right, she's the best boat. But if it's rough at the other end the boat sails back and forth at sea. She can't dock, lovey. That's the worst. Back and forth, all night.'

A fisherman enjoying a slice of partridgeberry pie and ice cream cast an eye at the patch of sky framed in the window. A fog horn mooed in the gloom. 'Ye'll be oll roight fer sailin',' he said, and went back to his slice of pie.

No one knows the sea better than a Newfoundland fisherman. We crossed on calm and peaceful waters. The cafeteria was now open, reminded the ferry crew. Happy fortieth birthday to Terry. The *Caribou* slid away from Port aux Basques towards Nova Scotia and the end of our Canadian journey – the end of our affair with the Beast. I felt as wistful as the last codfish in the sea.

'We'll be back,' said Ken.

Epilogue

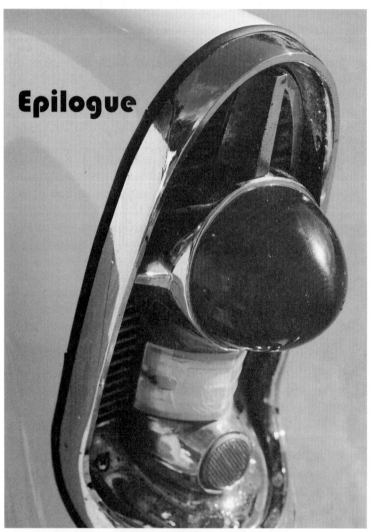

'You never really own a classic car.
You're only a custodian.'

Gerry, tow-truck driver, Halifax, Nova Scotia

Some free advice for anyone thinking of selling a car on the Internet: throw the laptop out the window and handcuff yourself to the nearest heavy object until the urge passes.

After the auction there was a suspicious silence from Okotoks. No jumping-for-joy emails, no bundles of money winging their way to Bruce, no phone calls imploring us to send the car of his dreams right now. Ken phoned Okotoks Man. Okotoks Man had a problem with Okotoks Woman. She was highly displeased, or earthier words to that effect. Okotoks Man might have to sleep in the back of the wagon. He asked more questions. Ken answered them. He wanted more photos. I sent them. Plainly, Okotoks Man rued that fateful bid-winning moment.

He rued it enough not to buy the car, in a Pythonesque series of events that saw us suspended from the Internet auction site and all but labelled fraudsters for unwittingly breaking the rules by selling a car registered to somebody else, even with that somebody else's full blessing. It'd been much easier dealing with a tattooed Czech ex-gangster in a Roman campground.

Luckily, Serious Chevy Buyer still wanted the car, despite stern warnings about our unsavoury character. Then the Cellphone That Never Rang rang. Serious Chevy Buyer? No, Saskatoon Chevy Fan. He'd been thinking it over. He wanted the car. Fergawdsake. For a microsecond the scales tipped in his favour. Maybe we could negotiate visiting rights to the Beast. But Serious Chevy Buyer stepped up to the mound.

Our Beast, our old, trusty, well-travelled Chevy, was sold.

Not quite, of course. There was paperwork to sort out, phone calls to make to Bruce, promises of rewards if he'd send on the money.

'Don't you trust me?' said Bruce. 'I did see a nice '54 Oldsmobile convertible online.'

The Beast had carried us through six time zones and all ten Canadian provinces, some more than once. Clocking up nineteen thousand kilometres in three months, with scarcely a moment to rest its springs, might have been asking far too much from an old jalopy approaching its fiftieth birthday. But the moose moments more than made up for the pack of flat coyotes. Already plans were afoot for another Newfoundland trip in search of spring icebergs afloat with seal hitchhikers – but not by classic car.

We gave away all the Beast's trappings: mattress, duvets, mosquito net (never used), tool kit (used only to crack lobsters), socket set (never used). Ken badly wanted the socket set. He put it in his suitcase, took it out. Weighed it, put it in, took it out.

'I bought a painted starfish instead of a fishing buoy and now you're thinking about taking a forty-pound socket set back with you?'

The socket set stayed behind.

On a wet grey afternoon the Beast rolled on to a transporter truck for the second time in its Canadian life. The car would travel first by truck, then by rail, to its new home in St Thomas, the Ontario town where Jumbo the circus elephant had run away and got hit by a train. P. T. Barnum dragged poor Jumbo's stuffed carcass around for years. Our Beast wouldn't be so foolish.

Like so many Canadians, from west to east, from the mountains to the sea, Gerry the truck driver loved classic cars. As I snuffled and dabbed at my eyes with a tissue he offered a word of comfort. 'You never really own a classic car. You're only a custodian.'

Then he got in his truck and ferried our Beast away.

A few weeks later the new custodians sent an email. The Beast had arrived in good condition. It had a new home and a new name.

Kiwi.

Back to life in small scenic New Zealand, back to another lazy summer in which to regain the use of legs and reshape bench-seat-flattened bottoms. Back to being boring Toyota owners.

'I miss the Chevy,' Ken said often.

I did, too. Camping in a Hiace van was about as thrilling as sleeping in a tool shed.

Not put off by our online travails Ken trawled Trade Me for another motorbike to add to his collection. Or so I thought.

'Look at this,' he said one day. 'It's a '56 Chevy 210 Townsman station wagon. It's here, in the North Island. I might email this ad to Bruce. Waddaya reckon?'

This Chevy was a pretty robin's-egg blue. In every other way it looked just like ours. For a full minute I gazed at that smiley chrome grille, the curve of fender and fin.

Then I threw the laptop out the window and fetched the handcuffs.

The Author

Karen Goa is an Auckland-based travel and food writer and co-author of the travel book *Bitten by the Bullet: Motorcycle Adventures in India.* When not barging around the planet on motorbikes or in classic cars she is also a medical writer, general journalist and fiction writer. If you'd like to contact the author with thoughts on travel, food or life on wheels please email kgoa@kiwilink.co.nz